# GENDER ROLE IN COMMUNICATION STYLE

**About the Author**

**Vijai N. Giri,** Ph.D. in Interpersonal Communication, is an Assistant Professor in the Department of Humanities & Social Sciences, Indian Institute of Technology, Kharagpur. He is recipient of many awards and distinctions including National Merit Scholarship and the prestigious German Academic Exchange Service (DAAD) Long-Term Fellowship.

Dr. Giri has participated and presented papers in a number of national and international conferences and has published two book chapters. He has published a dozen of research articles in national and international journals of repute. He has also worked as the guest editor of *International Journal of Communication*. Dr. Giri organizes short-term training programmes on *Interpersonal Communication* for college teachers and middle level managers. His current research interests include interpersonal communication, communication styles, intercultural communication, gender studies, and conflict management.

# GENDER ROLE IN COMMUNICATION STYLE

VIJAI N. GIRI
Department of Humanities and Social Sciences
Indian Institute of Technology, Kharagpur (W.B.)

*Foreword by*

B.N. PUHAN
Vice-Chancellor
North Orissa University

CONCEPT PUBLISHING COMPANY, NEW DELHI-110059

**Cataloging in Publication Data—DK**
Courtesy: D.K. Agencies (P) Ltd. <docinfo@dkagencies.com>

**Giri, Vijai N.,** 1960-
Gender role in communication style / Vijai N. Giri ; foreword by B.N. Puhan.
p. cm.
Includes bibliographical references.
Includes index.
ISBN 81-8069-133-0

1. Sex role. 2. Communication. 3. Interpersonal communication. I. Title.

DDC 305.3 21

ISBN 81-8069-133-0

First Published 2004



*Published and Printed by*
Ashok Kumar Mittal
**Concept Publishing Company**
A/15-16, Commercial Block, Mohan Garden
NEW DELHI - 110059 (India)

*Phones* : 25351460, 25351794
*Fax* : 091-11-25357103
*Email* : publishing@conceptpub.com

To

***MY WIFE***
***PUSHPA***

# FOREWORD

The selection of 'communication' as the central theme of research presented in this book is very timely. Today the importance of communication skills is felt in all walks of life. As our society is changing very fast, the ideas and cultural values of men and women are also changing which are reflected in their communication styles. The knowledge of effective communication styles has become an essential for success.

The present book deals with gender role, self-disclosure, self-esteem, and communication styles. The work is ambitious and the strength of the study lies in the fact that the author has rigorously examined the role of 'individual difference variables' as mediators of communication styles. The study is well-designed and the data are competently analysed. The role of gender in communication is rightly included, as previous results are full of contradictions. Self-disclosure is associated with communication styles. Self-disclosure lies at the heart of the process of interpersonal communication. Variation in self-esteem may change our communication style. All the variables have been very carefully explained and thoroughly examined. The findings are quite informative. It has been found that 'masculine' individuals with high self-disclosure and high self-esteem tend to have noble communication style, whereas 'feminine' individuals with low self-disclosure and low self-esteem tend to have reflective communication style.

It is important to note that managers, students, teachers, and other professionals working in the area of interpersonal communication may be greatly benefited by the major observations of the author. While conducting seminars on communication skills, trainers may emphasize that effective communication is not based on biological sex; rather it is based on gender role, self-disclosure, and self-esteem of a person. Our communication pattern with others is deeply rooted in our self-esteem. We can learn more effective techniques while giving presentations, writing memos, and conducting meetings by understanding properly the communication behaviours of individuals based on their gender roles. Communication style is learned; it is not a personality trait that will never change. Each style is simply different from the others and has good and bad characteristics. One can learn and develop these communication styles to make a difficult task easy.

These findings are also useful in interpersonal relations. Many scholars have observed that women and men have different ways of talking. If a person is aware of sex, gender role, and communication style while interacting with others, chances of misunderstanding become less. People having problems in communicating with each other, for example, married couples, students and teachers, father and son, boss and subordinates, etc. may easily benefit by understanding properly the sex and gender role of individuals.

I am sure that the readers of this book will find its contents quite interesting and the researchers in the area of gender and communication will imbibe fresh ideas from the work. It will give a new direction to further researches in the area of interpersonal communication in India. Dr. V. N. Giri must be congratulated on his pioneering attempts to analyse gender role and its effect on the communication styles of Indian college students.

I am confident that this book will be highly appreciated amongst scholars working in the area of communication and will prove to be a practical book for many to improve their knowledge in communication skills.

August 26, 2003

**B.N. Puhan**
*Vice-Chancellor*
North Orissa University

# PREFACE

In today's challenging world, the need for effective communication abilities is universally felt. Communication skills have become an integral part of most of the professional courses all over the world. Leaders, social workers, teachers, managers, businesspersons and the common people realize that the knowledge of effective communication styles is essential for peaceful and successful professional and social lives.

The book has been organized in five chapters. Chapter one describes in detail the researches on gender and communication. The construct of communication style has long been a topic of interest among scholars. The different communication styles that a person adapts in different situations have been discussed. Self-disclosure lies at the heart of the process of interpersonal communication. It gives an important indication by which others know what is going on inside the communicator. The findings based on self-disclosure and communication provides avenues for further thinking in this area. Self-esteem concerns the value we place on the images we have of ourselves. If we add to our self-description that we feel pleased about our career and family responsibilities, and are not disappointed in dealing with difficulties, we are referring to self-esteem. To a significant degree, self-esteem is influenced by evaluative information received from others. Self-esteem is developed in women and men through their experiences and interactions with others and through cultural messages. It is a personality variable that will greatly affect the way a person receives and reacts to a message. Change in self-esteem may result in changes in our communication behaviours. Thus, the impact of self-esteem on communication styles has been examined.

Chapter two describes the sample characteristics, measures and the test administration. Data were collected using four measures: Bem Sex Role Inventory, Communication Style Profile Test, Masculine and Feminine Self-Disclosure Scale, and Rosenberg Self-Esteem Scale. The details of data collection and the test administration have been described in this chapter.

Chapter three contains the description of results. The data have been analysed by using suitable statistics and the findings have been reported. Chapter four deals with the discussion of the findings. The limitations and suggestions for future research have been discussed in this chapter. Finally, in chapter five a brief summary of the work has been presented for a quick look and absorption.

This book is my humble effort in the area of gender role and communication. I shall be highly rewarded if this book offers some new ideas and directions to those who are interested in teaching and research in interpersonal communication.

**Vijai N. Giri**

August 18, 2003

## ACKNOWLEDGEMENTS

I express my deep sense of gratitude to Dr. M.B. Sharan, Professor of Psychology, for his valuable advice at various stages of writing. I am grateful to Professor B.N. Puhan, Vice-Chancellor, North Orissa University for writing the Foreword for this book. I feel highly obliged to Dr. H.R. Tewari, Professor of Sociology and Head, Department of Humanities and Social Sciences, who was always a source of encouragement to me. His readiness to provide all possible help in the hour of need was a great stimulus to me.

I am indebted to Dr. B.P. Sandilya, Professor of English, for his help in going through the manuscripts of the book and giving his suggestions. My heartfelt thanks go to my colleagues, Dr. M.K. Mandal, Professor of Psychology, for his help, suggestion and moral support in completing this work, and to Dr. D. Suar, Associate Professor of Psychology, for his critical evaluation and comments.

My thanks are also due to Prof. S. Srinivasan, Prof. Bani Chatterjee, Prof. P. Basu, Dr. Manasi Sinha, Dr. Anjali Roy, Dr. Abha Chatterjee, Dr. K.B.L. Srivastava and other colleagues in the Department for providing all sorts of help and encouragement. I wish to acknowledge the kind cooperation of Prof. Anil Kumar who provided me all necessary help in collecting data. I am also thankful to Ipsita Das and Trupti Mishra, research scholars of the Department, for their assistance. I must thank Dr. M. Venkatesan who helped me whenever required. I also appreciate Mr. Kishore Kumar's painstaking effort in typing my scribble into legible matter. I am thankful to all my colleagues and friends in the Department and in the Institute who were always ready to extend any kind of help I needed in completing this book.

I would like to acknowledge the support provided by the members of my family. I am greatly indebted to my father for his constant inspiration who is no more to see the completion of this book. My mother has always been a great source of encouragement to me. It is because of her blessings that I could complete this book. I am proud of my sons, Manish Kumar Giri (Vikki) and Ambarish Kumar Giri

(Ambar), who freed me from my responsibilities to them so that I could concentrate fully on my work. I am grateful to my wife who has always been an inspiring presence behind every stage in carrying out this work.

Finally, I would like to mention here that I have taken help from many books and journals in writing this book. I am grateful to all those authors and publishers whose works were found to be very useful and have been cited in this book. My special thanks are due to Prof. L. McCallister, Prof. S. Bem, and Prof. J. B. Weaver for their valuable comments and advice. I am extremely grateful to Mr. Ashok Kumar Mittal, Publisher, Concept Publishing Co. for his kind support and interest in publishing this book.

**Vijai N. Giri**

September 8, 2003

# CONTENTS

# LIST OF TABLES

# LIST OF FIGURES

# 1

# INTRODUCTION

We are living in an age which is full of challenges and competitions. To the best of our capabilities, we try to meet these challenges. A person might possess a number of good qualities necessary for dealing with various problems of daily life, but lack of effective communication abilities might make the task difficult. Today, it cannot be denied that an individual's success or failure largely depends on his/her communicative abilities.

Over the past two decades, considerable research attention has been focused on gender differences in communication. Our society is changing rapidly in attitudes and values, and this has prompted individuals to converse freely about issues related to men and women. In this context, religion, culture and attitudes of individuals have been found playing an important role in understanding the behaviour of men and women. Keeping this in mind, the present study purports to explore the impact of certain personality characteristics on communication behaviour of men and women. Since very little attempt has been made to do research in this area in our country, this kind of research might be quite relevant and interesting to many of us.

We can make our lives easier by understanding properly the different communication styles that individuals adapt in different situations. Every culture prescribes different behaviours for males and females. These differences start early in their lives and continue throughout in one form or the other (Hoyenga & Hoyenga, 1979; Hyde & Rosenberg, 1980). In most cultures, it is generally observed that males are expected to be more aggressive, assertive and achievement-oriented, while females are expected to be more nurturant, sensitive and responsible (Whiting & Edwards, 1973). Each culture has a set of institutional structures and practices to teach sex roles. With the changing time, the socio-economic conditions of men and women are also changing. The effect of these changes is evident in the roles of males and females in our society which is clearly reflected in the communicative behaviours of both the sexes. In a cross-cultural study on sex role, Sethi and Allen (1996, p.107) have stated, "Indian women —even those with higher education and technical training—gravitate towards service profession, while their male counterparts are more likely to develop careers involving technical or political leadership. Perhaps Indian culture highly values a number of traits in both the sexes, but attributes higher status to a male displaying these traits".

In another study on the status of women and children in Indian society, it has been found that male children are more valued than female children, and they are socialized in different ways. Female children are still considered an economic liability to the family, not only until they are married but to some extent throughout their lives. The socialization process emphasizes modesty and adaptation for females, while it teaches male children to be aggressive, assertive, superior and independent (Baig, 1976; De Souza, 1975; Jain, 1975; Nanda, 1976). Further, Rao and Rao (1996) observed, "Although tremendous changes are taking place in India, they have left the institution of family untouched. People are still traditional and have not accepted egalitarian relations in the family" (p. 123).

Thus, it is clear that our society is changing very fast but the ideas and cultural values are not changing as rapidly as they appear to be. The present study investigates the current status of gender role, certain personality characteristics, and their impact on communication styles in college students in the rapidly changing Indian society.

Some researches in behavioural science suggest that the type of communication style chosen by an individual is determined by his or her personality factors. Therefore, this study proposes to examine certain personality variables like gender role self-perception, self-disclosure and self-esteem, which have been found to be related to communication. Thus, the study will address the following questions:

1. To what extent have the roles of men and women changed in our culture?
2. Do the biological sex and the gender role affect the communication styles of individuals?
3. To what extent do self-disclosure and self-esteem affect the communication styles of individuals?

## A Look at Human Communication

No man is an island. Interactions amongst human beings are inevitable. Many are the things we learn by interacting with each other. Communication is a process in social interaction. It is believed that in spite of good qualities, if a person is lacking good communication abilities, he/she cannot lead a meaningful and successful life. Since time immemorial, almost in all the cultures, the importance of communication has been emphasized for improving the quality of life. We often forget that we must work to make communication pleasant and effective. When we ignore important aspects of communication, we are inviting a number of problems in our daily lives ranging from hurt feelings between friends to wars between nations. We all appreciate a positive attitude, a glowing face and a captivating smile. All these can be learnt by practising the art of communication. Whether we are interacting with a corporate body, the academic world 6r with our friends and family members, communication skill is very much required for maintaining good relationship. Since success or failure in many careers and human endeavour is largely determined by how well one communicates, the subject of communication should be a vital part of our education. The knowledge of practical communication competence is an essential personal asset for teachers, social workers, businessmen, politicians and perhaps for people in all walks of life. Today, effective communication has become a prerequisite for success for everybody in this increasingly hectic and competitive world. As a result, researchers in this field have been trying to give new and better ideas to cope with the complex situation in our day-to-day lives.

### *Communication Defined*

Communication has been defined in several ways since people have different conceptions about it. The term 'communication' comes from the Latin word *communis* which means common. Communication refers to the commonness or sharing of information, ideas, facts, opinions, attitudes and understanding. Communication essentially means transmission of commonly meaningful information (Ghanekar, 1998).

Keith (1993) defines communication as "the transfer of information and understanding from one person to another person. It is a way of reaching others with facts, ideas, thoughts and values. It is a bridge of meaning among people so that they can share what they feel and know. By using this bridge a person can cross safely the river of misunderstanding that sometimes separates people" (p. 399).

One of the older 'classic' definitions of communication focuses on its interactional aspects. To Ruesch and Bateson (1951) communication includes "...all of those processes by which people influence one another. This definition is based on the premise that all actions and events have communicative aspects, as soon as they are perceived by a human being ... [and] that such a perception changes the information which an individual possesses and therefore influences him" (p. 6). Under this broad definition, every stimulus or event can have communicative significance. This would include words (verbal utterances) and actions (nonverbal factors). According to this definition, whenever we make an effort to influence another person, we are practising communication (Hunt, 1985).

In the view of Thayer (1963), communication occurs "whenever an individual assigns significance or meaning to an internal or external stimulus" (p. 43). This definition is consistent with the position taken by most communication theorists. The important notion here is that an individual stimulus has no inherent meaning. A word such as *Love* does not have 'meaning' itself. The word assumes whatever meaning it is assigned in the individual's mind. So, the exact meaning that a person assigns to *Love* may not be the same as that assigned by another. The difference in the assignment of meaning can create problems in interpersonal communication. A person may operate on one meaning for the word, based on his or her experience. His or her meaning may be different from that of others. In this way, when we begin to communicate, miscommunication is possible because of this difference (Hunt, 1985).

Scholars in the area of communication have given different definitions of communication, but a simple definition of communication presented by Miller (1951), puts it this way: "communication takes place when there is information at one place or person and we want to get it to another place or person" (p. 10). Verdman (1970) describes a design for effective communication and says, "Effective communication is purposive symbolic interchange resulting in workable understanding and agreement between the sender and the receiver" (p. 3).

Baird (1977) views communication as the process involving the transmission and reception of symbols eliciting meaning in the minds of the participants by making their life experiences common. From the management point of view, communication is best described as the means by which management gets its job done. Accordingly, communication can be defined as "purposive interchange of ideas, opinions, instructions, presented personally or impersonally by symbol or signal as to attain the goals of the organization" (Ghanekar, 1998, p. 5).

It has been observed that a great variety of definitions are available in literature on communication. Various writers, social scientists, mathematicians, statisticians, novelists, management associations, etc. have defined communication in so many ways that a standard definition of communication does not exist. Obviously, one need not wonder if communication is called as a 'chameleon word'—one that changes its meaning and application with each person who uses it.

The nature of communication is complex and its scope is very broad. If the study of communication were enlarged to provide a deep and insightful knowledge, it would include the entire gamut of psychological sub-disciplines, like perception, cognition, linguistics, motivation, etc. It would also extend into organizational areas such as structure, hierarchy, authority and management functions (Ghanekar, 1998). From these definitions one can conclude that:

1. Meaning is created and does not exist independent from the communicators. Meaning resides in the mind of each communicator.
2. Communication involves people. Since it is the individual who selects, transmits, and receives the messages, we have to think of communication as an important issue of human behaviour. Any discussion of communication must include the human element in order to be complete.
3. Communication stimuli can consist of almost everything within our environment. Because of this, we must develop respect for the complexity of the communication phenomenon. We must not take for granted that the information we transmit will be accurately and efficiently received by others.

### *Ancient Heritage for Communication Principles*

The ability to communicate well has always provided advantages to those who possess it. Communication has a rich history and its traditions can still be seen in modern day communication concepts. Much like life itself, communication is a process. That means, it is dynamic, ever-changing, and unending.

The ancient world, the East and the West, depended heavily on oral communication. For example, in ancient Greece and Rome, it was necessary to communicate well on one's feet when dealing with matters in government assemblies and courts of law. During the Medieval and Renaissance periods, the oral tradition continued. As writing became more important as a permanent record of communication, authors and books on written communication principles appeared.

Communication principles originated in the East. According to ancient Indian scholars, Sanskrit is supposed to be the oldest language popularly known as *Devvani,* which means it has originated directly from the mouth of God. For centuries it continued to be an oral language. In China, communication principles are based on and connected with the importance of bureaucratic traditions. For centuries, Chinese political theories were concerned with the problems of communicating within the vast government bureaucracy as well as between the government and the people. As early as the fourth century, these theorists were advising rulers and government officials. Their advice stated that information should flow smoothly upward and downward. The theorists also encouraged rulers and officials to minimize bias and falsification of sources and to resist the influence of cliques and opportunists (Krone, Garrett & Chen, 1992). Hence, some of today's principles of writing are founded on a mixture of ancient oral and written traditions.

### Interpersonal Communication

Before introducing the concept of interpersonal communication, it would be appropriate to emphasize the importance of *intrapersonal* communication. Communication is a two-way process that involves both sending and receiving messages. But it is not necessary that this process would require two participants. *Intrapersonal* communication takes place whenever we evaluate and react to internal and external stimuli. The first step towards effective communication with others is successful communication with ourselves. *Intrapersonal* messages reflect our physical self, emotional self, social self, self-concept, values, beliefs and attitudes—in short, our entire personality. Thus, the study of *intrapersonal* communication begins with knowing about ourselves. *Intrapersonal* communication is the foundation upon which interpersonal communication is based. Therefore, it is necessary to understand how we communicate with ourselves before we approach the process of communicating with others.

Interpersonal communication is one that takes place at least between two persons. It is characterized by active interaction. The quality of encounter and relationship that occurs between two people through such transaction determine the extent to which growth and development are enabled. Mutual trust, understanding and consideration grow out of positive interactions. In interpersonal communication, the major emphasis is on transferring information from one person to another. Communication is looked upon as a basic method of effecting behavioural change. Interpersonal communication refers to the exchange of messages between persons for constructing common meanings. It is important to note that the quality of a relationship is directly related to the quantity and quality of information sharing.

Interpersonal communication has a long history within the vast area of communication. In the early 1900s, Simmel (1950) was making astute observations about interpersonal communication that are still debated today—such as "reciprocal knowledge", "characteristics of the dyad", interaction "rituals", "secrecy", "lies and truths" and "types of social relationship".

Many intellectual seeds for the study of interpersonal communication were sown during the 1920s and 1930s. Elton Mayo and his colleagues at the Harvard Business School were uncovering the potential power of social interaction and social relationship in the work setting. In the 1940s and 1950s Eliot Chapple believed that the matching of interaction rhythms led to an impression of harmony, whereas mismatching signalled discord—regardless of the content. Anthropologists Birdwhistell (1952) and Hall (1959) were interested in the total process of communication, but their pioneering efforts and observations of body movement, gestures, postures, and the use of space laid the groundwork for the study called "nonverbal communication" predominantly examined as interpersonal behaviour.

In the late 1950s, Fritz Heider's book, *The Psychology of Interpersonal Relations* (1958) helped to launch a line of research on attribution theory that is integral to the study of interpersonal communication today. By the late 1970s, the study of interpersonal communication had established itself as a major area of study along with mass communication in the United States. This was not the case in Europe, Asia, and South America. Even today, interpersonal communication outside the United States is likely to be housed within psychology, sociology, or anthropology. The late 1980s and early 1990s seemed to be characterized by a tendency to embrace a variety of approaches to the study of interpersonal communication (e.g., quantitative and qualitative, micro and macro) to face difficult questions about what we know and how we know it (Knapp, Miller & Fudge, 1994).

The reason why many scholars study interpersonal communication is the hope to generate information that will improve social interaction and human relationships. They seek to uncover and articulate what might be termed "solutions" for communication problems. As a result, the literature in communication is now dotted with studies focusing on behaviours that are meant to enhance our close relationships and help us achieve our interpersonal goals (Vangelisti, 1998).

## *Review of Literature*

Literature related to the topic was collected from various available resources including libraries, requesting the authors for reprints and the internet. The empirical and theoretical studies were critically examined. The communication style being the dependent variable has been reviewed first followed by gender role self-perception, self-disclosure, and self-esteem.

## Communication Style

The construct of communication style has long been a topic of interest among scholars. During the Roman times, style was one of the "five canons of rhetoric" (Norton, 1983, p. 7) and Aristotle's observations and recommendations of speaking style are still found in the contemporary college textbooks. Currently, the way people perceive themselves interacting and communicating with others is called communication style (Norton, 1978, 1983).

Style refers to the way one communicates. Watzlawick, Beavin and Jackson's content and relational communication model (1967) defines the study of style, which focuses on the message's interpretation by the receiver and its impact on what is being said and how it is being said. Until recently, style has been studied more extensively by scholars outside the communication field than those within it (Pruett, 1989). Communication style is "the way one verbally, nonverbally, and paraverbally interacts to signal how literal meaning should be taken, interpreted, filtered, or understood" (Norton, 1983, p. 11). Tannen (1986) mentions that people have different conversational styles. So, when speakers from different parts of the country, or of different ethnic or class backgrounds, talk to each other, it is likely that their words will not be understood exactly as they were meant.

Norton (1978) identified nine different styles of communication. Norton's Communicator Style Scale (1983) examines nine variables: dominant, dramatic, contentious, animated, impression-leaving, relaxed, attentive, open and friendly. A dominant communicator takes charge of the conversation, while a contentious style is more argumentative. A dramatic communicator uses stories, metaphors, exaggerated movements, etc., while an animated style refers to the use of subtle nonverbal cues. A relaxed communicator shows low-tension levels, while an attentive communicator lets others know that he or she is listening. A person who readily reveals information about himself or herself is described as open, and a person who leaves an impact on the receiver's memory has used an impression-leaving style. The friendly style recognizes others positively. Further, Norton (1983) has concluded that these nine components actually reflect a single continuum ranging from non-directive communicative style through directive communicative style. The non-directive style embraces the attentive communicator who encourages, accommodates, and acknowledges others. On the other end of the continuum, the directive style involves the dominant communicator who talks frequently and takes control in social situations (Kirtley & Weaver, 1999).

Following a factor analysis of Norton's (1978) original inventory, Hansford and Hatti (1987) found an underlying structure defined by an attentive/supportive dimension and a dominant/animated dimension that paralleled the non-directive and directive communication styles. It is equally important that other researchers like Hart *et al.* (1980); O'Keefe (1988), have similar findings employing different operationalization of communication styles and methodologies.

The popular and well developed tools for exploring variations in the way people perceive themselves interacting with others is the Communication Style Profile Test (CSPT) by McCallister (1994). McCallister's conceptualisation of communication style, which appears to have evolved from the earlier work of Norton (1978) and Hart, Carlson, and Eadie (1980), involves three, rather than two, predominant styles that are labelled: Noble, Socratic and Reflective.

The Communication Style Profile Test is a series of sixty questions that measure how one communicates. It is said that people do not react to 'what' one says; instead, they react to 'how' one says what one says. Communication success is directly linked to other person's expectations which expect us to communicate just the way he or she communicates. One can learn to identify other people's expectations, to satisfy those expectations, and to control the outcome of any conversation. If one is attempting to get success or even just survive in today's challenging world, it is very important that he or she should be able to control what happens in the dyadic or group conversations. McCallister has provided an easy method for gaining this control. Emphasizing the importance of communication McCallister writes, "Communication. It can make or break a career, build or destroy a marriage, even begin or end a war. It is perhaps the most important thing we do. If we have a problem at work, we say it is a communication problem. If we have a problem in relationship, we say it is a communication problem. But we typically don't know how to fix these problems, and we often don't know what caused the problem" (McCallister, 1994, p. 3).

Because the present study aims at investigating the impact of gender role, self-disclosure and self-esteem on communication style as developed by McCallister (1994), it is desirable to discuss in some detail the three dominant communication styles—Noble, Socratic and Reflective. The Noble communicator is conceptualised as a direct and straightforward, who feels obligated to state the truth. A Socratic is a verbose, analytical communicator who is concerned with details, and a Reflective is a warm, supportive communicator who is concerned with interpersonal relations and the need to avoid conflict. Regarding the naming of these three dominant communication styles, McCallister states that to give equal importance to these styles the terms have been grounded in the rhetorical tradition. Noble is very Aristotelian, the Socratic is obviously akin to Socrates, and the Reflective is reminiscent of Plato.

Communication style is a matter of choice. No one style is better than the other ones. It is not something with which we are born and die. It is something that we learn and develop over time. Effective leaders develop the ability to use more than one style. It is not a personality trait that will never change. Everyone has the potential to use all three patterns of communication (i.e., Noble, Socratic, Reflective), but people tend to use one pattern predominantly (McCallister, 1994).

### *Noble*

The 'Nobles' are true believers who expect the personal feelings of the self to play a secondary role in the communication interaction. They believe that the primary purpose of communication is the exchange of information and honest opinions. Individuals who endorse the noble style rarely engage in personal self-disclosure, avoid lengthy discussion, argumentation and debate, expect yes-no responses, tend to be result-oriented communicator and are most concerned with the bottom line. Nobles' action-oriented style and desire to make quick decisions help them project an image of a powerful leader.

While Nobles have certain strengths, there are some weaknesses in their characteristics. The Nobles have a tendency to go from being assertive to turning aggressive. Aggressive communicative behaviours create a closed and defensive communication climate. Nobles expect everyone to be direct, straightforward, and totally honest, and this just isn't the way the world works and as a result they get frustrated (McCallister, 1994).

### *Socratic*

Socratics are individuals who are most concerned with rhetoric and the analysis of details and debates. They would openly engage in discussion, negotiation and arbitration. They are verbose, persuasive and argumentative. They are believed to see a holistic picture of communication and to have the ability and desire to sort through the gray areas to reduce hostility. Socratics have the potential to be successful problem solvers because of their ability to see issues from many perspectives. They use anecdotal stories and hypothetical examples to help the other person share or experience a similar moment in time.

Socratics also have got some weaknesses. They are very argumentative and the argumentative communication behaviours create a closed, defensive, and hostile communication climate. They have a tendency to be redundant, engage in non-stop conversations, as a result the other person stops listening to them. Socratics are poor listeners and have a tendency to interrupt the other person. Further, the directive and controlling nature of Socratics increases interpersonal conflict (McCallister, 1994).

### *Reflective*

Reflectives believe that the primary purpose of communication is the maintenance or advancement of personal relationship. The accurate transmission of information, expression of opinions, and tangible results play a secondary role in the communication encounter. They believe that the communication decorum should be polite and conflict-free. They try to maintain a warm, calm and supportive relationship. They often say what the other person wants to hear rather than what he or she really feels. They openly engage in personal self-disclosure, use verbal and nonverbal reinforcers to create a supportive climate. They are patient listeners, flexible and persuadable. They try their best to defuse communication hostility. They are soft-spoken and non-assertive. Reflectives have the ability to help other people solve their own problems; they tune into the needs of the other person and respect the confidential nature of the interaction.

Like other communicators, Reflectives too have got some weaknesses. They have a tendency to back away from controversial issues. They do not say what they really think and this causes personal frustration. The passive tendency causes the Reflectives to lose career opportunities because the other person views them as weak. They are verbally attacked because the other person knows the Reflectives will back down. They tend to be overly concerned with personal feelings and pleasant communication decorum, and this results in indecisiveness. Since they are indecisive and non-directive, they get prevented from achieving personal and professional goals. Reflectives are not viewed as credible communicators because of their soft-spoken, unassertive and non-committal style. As a tendency, they say what the other person wants to hear instead of what they really feel. This establishes them as dishonest or devious persons in the eyes of the other (McCallister, 1994).

Noble and Reflective communication styles articulated by McCallister appear consistent with the bifurcated conceptualisation proposed by others, but the Socratic style appears to be different (Kirtley & Weaver, 1999). Regarding sex differences in communication style, McCallister argues that communication style is acquired through socialization and the "sex-differences have absolutely nothing at all to do with communication style. Men don't tend to be one style and women another. Traditions and cultural mores may set up expectations regarding acceptable styles for women and acceptable styles for men, but biological gender does not cause women to be one style and men to be another" (McCallister, 1994, p. 203). She argues further that sex has also nothing to do with management or leadership abilities. No scientific research has suggested some genetic traits for men, which makes them better managers or leaders. Tradition and cultural mores may have placed men in these positions in the past, but these mores have been challenged, and the traditions are being broken. Sex-based style differences are myths. These stereotypical beliefs can be shattered if we look beyond sex and examine communication style as a cause of behaviours (McCallister, 1994).

A simple reason, which McCallister gives regarding sex differences in communication style, is traced to our traditions and cultures that are always in the process of change but have never been altogether eliminated. Thus, while male and female leadership behaviours may not differ, our expectations regarding acceptable behaviours from males and females may still differ. That is, what we expect and accept from men may be different from what we expect and accept from women. Of course, there are still some people who like certain behaviours in men and dislike the same behaviours in women and *vice versa*. Fortunately, the sex-based distinctions are gradually disappearing.

McCallister's conceptualisation of communication styles is based on more than a decade of research. McCallister worked with and tested thousands of students, workers, managers, and executives in an effort to develop a scale that will help the average person understand how communication can be used to improve one's life condition.

## Gender Role and Communication

The two terms, *sex* and *gender,* have been used in the present study with a very distinctive meaning. *Sex* refers to biological category, male and female, determined by the presence of XX chromosomes for females and XY chromosome pattern for males. *Gender*, on the other hand, is usually thought of as the learned behaviour a culture associates with being male or female. The ideal of masculinity is communicated to males, whereas the feminine ideal is communicated to females.

Ashmore and Del Boca (1979) reviewed the definition of sex stereotypes used by researchers and identified four generally accepted characteristics. A sex stereotype is usually considered to be cognitive; it is a set of beliefs, it deals with what men and women are alike, and it is shared by members of a particular group. The aspect of sex stereotypes such as sex trait stereotypes and sex role attitudes are closely linked. Sex trait stereotypes are the psychological characteristics and behaviour traits (masculine and feminine), which are believed to characterize men and women. Sex role is defined in terms of activities of social significance in which the two sexes participate with differential frequency. Sex stereotypes are the product of biological and social conditioning. Socialization for the development of appropriate sex traits and roles starts from childhood and passes through the phases of adolescence and adulthood. The different communication patterns of children and adults are caused by this socialization process (Das & Ghadially, 1996).

The origin of research on gender-related variables in communication probably can be traced to studies in which researchers included biological sex as a category to determine whether it affected the particular area of communication under consideration. Most of these studies treated biological sex as an accidental feature, rather than as the primary area of interest in the study (Ball, 1958; Bryan & Wilke, 1942). Further, these studies operated under a paradigm that suggested men and women were, indeed, different, and that we should expect to see differences in every instance (Pearson, West & Turner, 1995).

Some communication theorists have worked on constructs to provide a theoretical framework for organizing the sex and communication literature. Hart and his associates developed the Rhetorical Sensitivity construct (Hart & Burks, 1972; Hart, Carlson & Eadie, 1980) and defined the rhetorically sensitive person as one who characterizes herself or himself as a changing, fluctuating person who suitably adapts to the situational and environmental variations. Other researchers considered the importance of communication competence, which included an element of adaptability or flexibility (Bochner & Kelly, 1974; Cegala, 1981; Duran, 1992).

Gilligan (1982) suggests that based on different relationships with a female caregiver (mother), boys and girls develop psychologies and different ways of perceiving the world. By adulthood, the difference is maximized. Gilligan claims that men think in terms of vertical hierarchies and women in terms of horizontals and webs.

None of the theories discussed so far is satisfactory for understanding the communication behaviour we observe in males and females. However, researchers continue theorizing to gain a clearer understanding of gender and communication. Canary and Hause (1993) regarding researches on sex differences in communication state, "We believe that sex differences in communication do exist, but the ways in which researchers have conceptualized and operationalized sex have failed to elucidate these differences" (p.130). Researchers in the past three decades tried to examine biological sex differences in communication. During the first wave of research, a number of differences in communication were determined (Bostrom & Kemp, 1968). This work on sex differences in communication proceeded until 1974, when Bem (1974) introduced the concept of androgyny, the internalisation of both masculine and feminine characteristics. Androgyny has come from the Greek terms *andro* meaning male and *gyne* meaning female. This concept seemed to challenge the traditional category of masculine and feminine. In Bem's system, a person could be high or low in both masculinity and femininity as opposed to the older notion that high level of one would mean low level of the other. Bem (1993) described gender as a lens through which we view the world. She suggested that many of the choices we make about our own behaviour are to varying degrees guided by the cultural expectations for our gender.

Bem approached androgyny, masculinity and femininity as sex-roles or psychological orientations. Many researches, after 1974, replaced biological sex with psychological gender-role orientation (*cf.* Greenblatt, Hasenauer & Freimuth, 1980; Talley & Richmond, 1980). The Bem Sex Role Inventory (BSRI) (Bem, 1974) is the questionnaire most often used by researchers to measure masculinity, femininity and androgyny. The use of biological sex resulted in mixed findings, whereas the use of this new psychological gender instrument appeared to clarify the findings and sharpen the issue. In spite of several studies done in the area of gender and communication, the very basic question about women's and men's communication remains controversial even today.

Kirtley and Weaver (1999) argued that gender role self-perception is the key factor underlying our attitudes, beliefs and behaviours when interacting and communicating with others. Our perception of gender role is the result of the socialization process (Bandura, 1986; Eagly, 1987; Wood, 1994; Wood & Lenze, 1989). The applicability of the gender role self-perception concept in understanding communication phenomenon is suggested by several authors (Bem, 1976, 1981, 1985; Leaper, 1987; Lindsey & Zakahi, 1998). Individuals, whether male or female, who endorsed masculine gender role self-perception shared more verbal assertiveness and used more direct statements. Individuals who identified with the feminine gender role self-perception, on the other hand, used more personal references and were found more likeable (Leaper, 1987). In another study, Weaver, Fitch-Hauser, Villaume and Thomas (1993) explored the impact of masculine *versus* feminine gender roles on communication apprehension. They found that masculine individuals reported experiencing significantly less communication apprehension than their feminine counterparts. Significant sex differences were also evident, but the variance explained by sex differences, especially when compared with the effect size for gender role orientation proved to be very small.

The salience of the concept of gender makes many introduce the concept as a central variable in communication study. While some on the empirical periphery continue to castigate gender communication research, the area receives increasing attention from scholars in a variety of disciplines. We now live in a culture that views gender as integral to understanding human behaviour (Pearson, West & Turner, 1995).

A variety of models have guided the research on gender and communication. The initial lack of investigations on women promoted stereotypical images and effective communication models derived from the interactions of men. Implicitly, communicative success was equated with male practice. The communicative behaviours of both women and men are now examined with behavioural research replacing "folk linguistics". When we learn that a friend or acquaintance has been blessed with a baby, what is the first question we are likely to ask about the infant? When we see a person walking on the street ahead of us and cannot determine his/her biological sex immediately, why do we strive to find out if it is a man or woman? When we learn that an individual has made an important discovery, are we not curious to know if he/she is a male/female? Everyday we consider and ask questions about people's biological sex.

We make observations and predictions about whether people are male or female based on their communicative behaviour and their roles in the society. While gender and communication are intimately related, the relationship is not as simple and straightforward as it once might have been. Our society is changing; therefore, it is no longer easy to predict a person's occupation or family role based on his/her sex. For example, women are becoming increasingly successful in managerial roles and are attaining high status in a variety of organizations and fathers are becoming more involved with their children from the moment of birth.

The changing roles of women and men are inescapable, and the topic of gender and communication is relevant because of these vast sociological and psychological changes. Virtually every medium—books, magazines, newspapers, film, television, and radio carries stories about the changeable issues of man and woman's role and the manner in which they communicate with each other.

A considerable amount of research has attempted to understand the nature of various sex-roles and the ways these roles are interpreted and communicated. Researches on gender and communication are done mainly for two reasons. First, it helps us to understand in a better way the nature of our own human condition and how it makes a sense of the world in which we live. Second, from this understanding, we attempt to predict how better to live in our complicated and continually changing world. Thus, such type of research is of immediate and personal concern to many of us.

Tannen (1990) in her provocative and fascinating book suggests that we can make our lives a bit easier by becoming more aware of gender-based communication style. That way, we can make allowances rather than take disparities personally. If we have sense for the ways in which talk gets us into trouble—we can recognize our own conversations and misunderstandings.

If we understand the gender-based communication, we can, to some extent, avoid the misunderstanding in the way men and women talk to one another. No doubt, this field is very controversial. Some people become agitated as soon as they hear a reference to gender. A few become angry at the mere suggestion that women and men are different. And this reaction can come from either women or men. Despite these dangers, researches on gender and language are growing, because the risk of ignoring differences is greater than the danger of naming them. Denying real differences can only compound the confusion that is already widespread in this era of shifting and reforming relationships between women and men (Tannen, 1990).

Since long, researchers in the area of gender and communication have been arguing that men and women differ greatly in the way they communicate and interact with others (Aries, 1987; Kramarae, 1989; Lakoff, 1975; Tannen, 1990). Although there are differences but considerable research suggests that sex differences may play only a small role in the cognitive and behavioural processes that underlie communication (Eagly, 1987; Wood & Lenze, 1989).

Researches in this field often argue that language is not sex-neutral, it seems to divide, separate, and differentiate women from men (Doyle & Paludi, 1991). The separation between male and female as a simple dichotomy prevails in many cultures as it is evident, for example, from the Chinese *Yang* and *Yin*, the Hindu *Lingam* (*Shiva)* and *Yoni* (*Shakti*), and the Tantric Buddhist *Jewel* and *Lotus* (Bakan, 1966).

Individuals learn to be male or female by learning effective means of communications and social behaviours, which are required for their gender. In India, sex role is strongly related with the prevailing culture. Religion, culture and tradition have deep roots and have significant influence on the individual's personality and behaviour. Parents, siblings, and other members of the extended family, along with cultural mores, have a significant role in the timing, techniques, and emphasis on sex role development and training (Nyrop, Benderly, Cover, Cutter & Parker, 1975). Nyrop *et al.* (1975) observe that currently in India, the industrialization and migration have brought about some obvious changes in stereotyped concepts of masculinity and femininity affecting such factors as household composition, residence patterns, sleeping arrangements, specific kinship relationship, and male and female attitudes and behaviours. In a study of sex role attitudes, marriage and career among Indian college men and women, Ghadially and Kazi (1980) have provided evidence, which suggests that the role played by males and females in Indian society is gradually changing. Findings indicate a significant difference between 'traditional' and 'non-traditional' males and females on the above issues.

Tannen (1990, p. 42) suggests that "if women speak and hear a language of connection and intimacy, while men speak and hear a language of status and independence, then communication between men and women can be like cross-cultural communication, prey to a clash of conversational styles. Instead of different dialects, it has been said, they speak different *genderlects*". She states further that men's conversations are negotiations in which people try to achieve and maintain the upper hand if they can, and protect themselves from others' attempts to put them down and put them around. Conversations that women have are negotiations for closeness in which people try to seek and give confirmation and support.

Briton and Hall (1995) found that women were expected by members of both sexes to display greater skill at sending and receiving nonverbal messages. In this case, the researchers expected to find such differences since women have been observed to use certain non-verbal expressions more than men and were found to be better interpreters of facial expressions. Women are also accepted generally as better listeners than men (Marche & Peterson, 1993).

Perhaps, of all socio-demographic variables in communication, gender has been the most predominantly studied. In studying gender, one important thing researchers have emphasized, is the cultural difference. Singh and Lele (1990) point out that attention should be paid to the cultural differences in gender-power hierarchies. Where a number of scholars argue that there are gender differences in the communication pattern, D. Maccoby and Jacklin (1974), and Block (1976), in a monumental narrative review of literature, concluded that there are few sex differences and that those that do emerge are small in magnitude and often overshadowed by interactions. Thus, D. Maccoby and Jacklin suggested that females were not more social than males, were not better at simpler tasks, did not have lower self-esteem, and were not more suggestible than males. Zimbardo (1977) also did not find any evidence to support the cultural assumption that females are more shy than males. Hyde and Linn (1988) state, "our meta-analysis provides strong evidence that the magnitude of the gender difference in verbal ability is currently so small that it can effectively be considered to be zero. More detailed analysis of various types of verbal ability (e.g., vocabulary, reading comprehension, and analogies) similarly yielded no evidence of substantial gender difference" (p. 64).

But recent socio-linguistic researches in various cultures have found gender differences in the speech styles of adults (e.g., Philips, Steele & Tanz, 1987; Thorne, Kramarae & Henley, 1983). From this Sheldon (1993) expects that language is a major influence on what and how children learn about gender and that gender is a major influence on the way children use language in everyday life. Language functions not only to initiate novices but also to perpetuate and enforce asymmetrical gendered behaviour by means of reconstructing social relations between and among females and males in countless ordinary daily conversations over a lifetime.

There are gender differences in ways of speaking and we need to identify and understand them. Without such understanding, we are doomed to blame others, or ourselves or the relationship. Talk between women and men is like cross-cultural communication. A cross-cultural approach to gender differences in conversational style differs from the work on gender and language, which claims that conversations between men and women break down because men seek to dominate women. Tannen (1990) states that "no one could deny that men as a class are dominant in our society and that many individual men seek to dominate women in their lives. And yet male dominance is not the whole story. It is not sufficient to account for everything that happens to women and men in conversations—especially conversations in which both are genuinely trying to relate to each other with attention and respect. The effect of dominance is not always the result of an intention to dominate" (p. 18).

Gender role is usually thought of as learned behaviour. The ideals of masculinity is communicated to males, whereas, the feminine ideals are communicated to females. Often this process fuses sex and gender together, although theoretically they are separate concerns. Some commentators argue that it is as if males and females have been raised on two different planets or at least, two different cultures, with two unique patterns of communicating (Gray, 1992). Numerous scholars in the area of gender and communication have observed the stereotypical role of male and female. Females have been characterized as emotional, passive, gentle, highly talkative and having an abundance of facial expressions. Males, on the other hand, have been characterized as task-oriented, blunt, aggressive, ambitious and independent (Canary, Emmers-Sommer & Faulkner, 1997; Deaux & Lewis, 1983; Doyle & Paludi, 1991; Hall, 1984; Kramarae, 1989; Lott, 1987; Lindzey & Aronson, 1985; Tannen, 1990).

Montgomery and Norton (1981) focused specially on communication styles and proposed, "a large but fragmented body of literature suggests that men and women differ significantly in their interpersonal communication" (p. 122). Burleson and Samter (1992) also found sex differences to be significant in social participation and communication skills. Heiss (1991), contrary to stereotypic beliefs, found that male and female displayed equal power and dominance through their communication styles in intimate relationships. Wheelen and Verdi (1992) found no stereotypic sex differences in the categories of task, maintenance, or verbal participation. Simkins-Bullock and Wildman (1991) also found that sex differences did not explain substantial differences in the type of language incorporated in the communication styles of males and females. A meta-analysis conducted by Lustig and Andersen (1990) found no sex difference in the communication pattern.

Thus, the studies on gender and communication are full of contradictions. Researchers have always been trying to put forward their views by using different methodologies and philosophies.

## Self-Disclosure and Communication

In general terms, self-disclosure has been defined as "any information exchange that refers to the self, including personal states, dispositions, events in the past, and plans for the future" (Chelune, 1979, p. 152). A large amount of work has used a similar definition and focused on self-disclosure as a relational development mechanism especially in terms of reciprocity. Self-disclosure means the intentional sharing of intimate information about one's self with others. It is practised in an effort to make oneself known honestly to another. This process is self-presentational and instrumental in the management of interpersonal relationships.

Self-disclosure involves individuals conveying information about themselves to others that the other people do not know (Altman & Taylor, 1973). Usually, self-disclosure is associated with direct communication styles that predominate in individualistic cultures, rather than with the indirect communication styles that predominate in collectivistic cultures (Gudykunst & Ting-Toomey, 1988). It is observed that individualists would engage in more self-disclosure than would collectivists. Barnlund's (1975) research in Japan and the United States supports this contention. Culture has also a great impact on self-disclosure. Barnlund (1975) contends that "the greater the cultural homogeneity, the greater the meaning conveyed in a single word, the more that can be implied rather than stated" (p. 162). This implies that explicit self-disclosure is not needed to convey intimate information. Gudykunst, Yoon and Nishida (1987) found that the greater the degree of collectivism present in a culture, the greater the differences between ingroup (i.e., classmate) and outgroup (i.e., stranger) communication in terms of amount of personalization (e.g., intimacy of communication) and synchronization (i.e., coordination of communication) and of difficulty in communication.

Self-disclosure lies at the heart of the process of interpersonal communication. It gives an important indication by which others know what is going on inside the communicators. Of course, self-disclosure is not always easy. Our natural tendency is to hide feelings of incompetency, loneliness, guilt, worries over love and rejection, conflicts over anger and resentment towards loved ones. Even when the feelings involved are not intense, self-disclosure may still be difficult, because of well-learned habits that help us to avoid emotional hurt. In our society, it is observed that people are accustomed to hiding what they really want, think, or feel. This may affect our communication styles. Confiding in others and receiving their confidence is, therefore, one of the most effective interpersonal communication tools (Barker, 1978).

Self-disclosure has been most widely researched so far as the talking behaviour of individuals is concerned. Initially, researchers assumed that revealing intimate information about oneself was healthy, fostering favourable impressions and relationship development. (See, for example, Jourard & Friedman, 1970; Worthy, Gary & Kahn, 1969). Later investigations have questioned the generality of these phenomena. The dynamics of self-disclosure processes appear to be influenced by a host of factors including norms, valence, topic, relationship among interactants, setting and other language variables (Bradac, Hosman & Tardy, 1978; Gilbert, 1976; Tardy, Hosman & Bradac, 1981).

The main issue in self-disclosure research focuses on the reasons why people do it. Duck and Pittman (1994) stated, "Jourard, a humanistic psychologist, the founding father of self-disclosure theory and research, felt that the primary goal of self-disclosure was the maintenance of one's mental health" (p. 687). Jourard (1971) says "self-disclosure is the act of making yourself manifest, showing yourself, so others can perceive you" (p. 19). Essentially, this makes self-disclosure a declarative, individually expressive act rather than a socially communicative one. Jourard's contention was that by self-disclosing to another, we are able to validate our thoughts and feelings and understand more fully how we conform to the world around us. For Jourard (1959), self-disclosure was a prerequisite for a healthy personality, but in real life, people may not have "reasons" like this or may have other reasons, embedded in the conversational realities of everyday life that tend to influence self-disclosing behaviour. Based on Jourard Self-Disclosure Questionnaire (JSDQ), several years of extensive research indicated that females disclose more than males (Dimond & Munz, 1967; Jourard & Lasakow, 1958). Later-borns disclose more than firstborns (Dimond & Hellkamp, 1969; Dimond & Munz, 1967). Although much of the research using the JSDQ has been contradictory, and it has been found to be a weak indicator for predicting specific acts of self-disclosure (Chelune, 1979, p. 4), it remains a strong prototype for researchers measuring individual self-disclosure characteristics.

The link between gender and self-disclosure has been perhaps the variable that has received the most attention in self-disclosure research over the past forty years. Originally, gender was seen as trait-like, with the idea that particular characteristics of gender would be consistent from situation to situation. However, it is now generally understood that there are mediating factors that require a more complex understanding of the role of gender and self-disclosure. There are several current studies that for the most part, remain true to traditional trait-like perspectives of self-disclosure (Duck & Pittman, 1994).

For example, Snell, Miller and Belk (1988) and Snell, Miller, Belk, Garcia-Falconi, and Hernandez-Sanchez (1989) examined the relationship between gender and self-disclosure, using a number of questionnaires similar to the original JSDQ. Subjects were asked to self-report anticipated levels of self-disclosure for specific disclosure recipients, female friends, male friends and spouses/lovers (Snell *et al.*, 1988) and mothers, fathers, a female therapist, and a male therapist (Snell *et al.*, 1989).

In examining various aspects of self-disclosure, Pearson, West and Turner (1995) have observed a general pattern that women self-disclose more, they are more aware of the cues that affect their self-disclosure. The reason given for this is, women may self-disclose more because they are socialized to be open and expressive, that is, our culture promotes self-disclosure among women, yet restricts this behaviour among men.

Why do women self-disclose more than men? Perhaps, self-disclosure is more important to women than men. One may also conclude that relationship is more important to women than men. Why this would be the case is not known but is still worth considering. Perhaps, our economic system has evolved in such a way that it forces women to assume subservient communication postures, that is, women disclose more because lesser status people always disclose more to high status persons than *vice versa*.

Thus, self-disclosure is paramount in the development of our healthy relationships. Self-disclosure appears to be a generally positive communication skill when it is understood and used in moderation.

When researchers study self-disclosure, they characterize it in many different ways. Four of the more common ways to understand self-disclosure are:

1. As an aspect of the personality, or an individual trait.
2. As an individual behaviour.
3. As a result of dyadic interaction.
4. As transformative.

The basic characteristic of self-disclosure as an interaction is that it occurs in a dyad. The earliest literature on self-disclosure discusses its "dyadic effect". The reference by Jourard suggests that self-disclosure occurs only in the dyad and a large number of studies have investigated it in this setting (Winstead, 1986; Zillman, Weaver, Mundorf & Aust, 1986). Researchers who have studied self-disclosure within the dyad have concluded that self-disclosure is generally reciprocal, that is, as the disclosure of one person increases, so does that of the other person (Feigenbaum, 1977).

Closely related to the reciprocal nature of self-disclosure is the relationship between self-disclosure and trust (McAlister, 1980). Individuals who trust each other are more likely to self-disclose than are individuals who do not. Trust exerts a strong influence on the willingness of both persons to disclose in a dyad. This feeling of trust might have roots in early childhood. People who felt that their parents were nurturing or high in affection tend to be more trusting and higher in self-disclosure (Pedersen & Higbee, 1969; Snoek & Rothblum, 1979).

The sex composition of the dyad makes a difference in self-disclosure behaviour. Winstead (1986, p. 93) observed, "the presence of a female has a powerful effect on the social behaviour of another, it makes him or her more self-disclosing, more open, and less lonely." Hacker (1981) noted that when men disclose to women they tend to confide their weaknesses while enhancing their strengths, to give a balanced view of strengths and weaknesses. When women disclose to men, they tend to conceal their strengths while confiding their weaknesses. In this disclosure pattern, men and women reinforce traditional sex-role stereotypes where men are in a dominant position compared to women (Pearson, West & Turner, 1995).

Based on different findings on self-disclosure, one can confidently say that self-disclosure has the ability to change relationship and relationship matters a lot in human communication behaviours. A pattern in self-disclosure seems to emerge in relationships between non-strangers. First, a relatively high level of non-intimate information is disclosed, and then intimate information is disclosed at a gradually increasing rate (Taylor, 1965). The least amount of self-disclosure may occur between acquaintances who do not know each other very well, but between whom future interactions are likely to occur (Pearce & Sharp, 1973). The length of the relationships also affects self-disclosure.

Researchers also indicate the influence of self-disclosure on friends. Disclosure with female friends usually focuses on person or family topics, and these topics are more emotional in nature (Haas & Sherman, 1982). Pearson (1993) reported that college students disclose more to their best same-sex friend than to either one of their parents. Disclosures between male-male friendships were originally studied by Tiger (1969). Tiger believed that men form some sort of bond that is linked to them being male. Males find it difficult to reveal their emotions (Derlega, Metts, Petronio & Margolis, 1993) and are taught to hold back their emotional experiences (Doyle, 1991; Herzberger & Tennen, 1985; Lewis, 1986).

Family relationships have also been examined for patterns of self-disclosure. In general, children of either sex tend to self-disclose more to their mothers than to their fathers (Balswick & Balkwell, 1977; Jourard & Lasakow, 1958). However, fathers appear to be the recipients of more accurate disclosures (Woodyard & Hines, 1973). If the various aspects of self-disclosure are examined, it becomes obvious that women self-disclose more, are disclosed more and are more aware of cues that affect their self-disclosure. High self-disclosure of women may be because of the socialization process. They are socialized to be open and expressive, that is, our culture promotes self-disclosure among women.

Independent of biological sex, self-disclosure is also explained by examining the psychological gender. Greenblatt, Hasenauer and Freimuth (1980) demonstrated that masculine men have lower total disclosure scores than androgynous men, but that feminine females do not report higher total disclosure scores than androgynous women. Pearson (1980) found that masculine females disclosed more than feminine females, and feminine males disclosed more than masculine males.

Based on information available on self-disclosure and as a consequence of the positive attitude towards self-disclosure, practitioners have encouraged the communication behaviour in a variety of ways. Self-disclosure is identified as a dimension of interpersonal competence (Bochner & Kelly, 1974), and as a component of dialogue (Johannesen, 1971). Tannen (1990) and Maccoby (1990) acknowledge that men and women grow up and live in different 'subcultures'; as a result they have two different perspectives on the self-disclosure process. Self-disclosure plays an important role in the communication styles of individuals. The basic purpose of self-disclosure may be gaining information about other persons and is one way to learn about how another person thinks and feels. Various researches have tried to find out how self-disclosure affects the lives of mankind. Self-disclosure is possibly a give-and-take business. If someone's goal is to get the other to disclose information, he/she may start the conversation by disclosing information, thereby making the other person feel a sense of obligation to reciprocate and also disclose information. Although there are risks in this process, the benefits outweigh those risks by achieving an intimate and loving relationship with other. Without self-disclosure, participating in a relationship would prove to be difficult, if not impossible.

Instructional communication researchers have identified a wide variety of teacher-student relationships. Teacher's use of communication behaviours such as communicator styles (Norton, 1977, 1978, 1983, 1986; Nussbaum & Scott, 1979) and self-disclosure (Nussbaum & Scott, 1979) have been linked to students' effective and cognitive learning outcomes. Feeney, Noller and Callan (1994) found that security of attachment was associated with greater and more responsive self-disclosure, more compromising and integrating styles of problem solving, and less rejecting and more supportive interpersonal interaction.

Communication usually qualifies as self-disclosure when one individual reveals information about the self to another during face-to-face interaction (Duck, Rhutt, Hurst, & Strejc, 1991; Parker & Parrott, 1995; Petronio, 1991). "Self-disclosure is generally regarded as a process in which relationships proceed from non-intimate to intimate areas of exchange with regard to content" (Gilbert & Horenstein, 1975, p. 317).

The relationship-oriented communication style and high level of self-disclosure is common among women (Aries, 1987; Tannen, 1990). Tannen (1986) states that self-disclosure and shared values are essential to intimacy and are deeply influenced by cultural and ethnic norms. Ethnic groups can be characterized by the way they value and express self-disclosure. Thus, through survey of literature it becomes obvious that self-disclosure has a great impact on an individual's communication style.

## Self-Esteem and Communication

Self-esteem concerns the value we place on the images we have of ourselves. If we add to our self-description that we feel pleased about our career and family responsibilities, and are not disappointed in dealing with difficulties, then we are referring to self-esteem. To a significant degree, self-esteem is influenced by evaluative information received from others (Pearson, West & Turner, 1995).

Self-esteem is developed in women and men through their experiences and interactions with others and through cultural messages. Men and women may learn how valuable they are through their relative visibility in language.

Researchers have always been interested in examining self-esteem. Much of an individual's self-esteem is a result of how women and men define themselves. Josephs, Markus and Tafarodi (1992) reported that typically, women are more likely to have a "collectivist, ensembled, or connected" schema for their selves, whereas men are more likely to develop an "individualistic, independent or autonomous" scheme for their selves. These orientations influence the value that is placed on the images we have of ourselves.

In her book on self-esteem, Steinem (1992) noted that in her travels, she encountered so many women who were "smart, courageous and valuable [and yet], who did not think they were smart, courageous or valuable" (p. 3). She claimed that women are often the targets of self-help materials, which offer ways to improve self-esteem. DeFrancisco and Allison (1992) explained this trend by noting, "women's self-esteem is portrayed as women's fault and women's responsibility to correct" (p. 5).

Lott (1987) and Miller (1986) argued that in a powerless societal position, women find themselves responsive to the prevailing masculine way of thinking and doing. Lott specifically noted that low self-esteem in women is also a "predictable consequence of women's socialization, since girls learn early that they will be less important, less powerful, and less effective than men" (p. 246). Women and men's self-esteem may also be affected by others' perceptions of their own worth. With these findings, it can be said that our society, in general, values men more than women, and the differences are expected in male's and female's self-esteem. However, this is not always the case. Although there is a tendency for males to have a stronger sense of self-worth, the difference is slight and the findings are mixed (Pearson, West & Turner, 1995).

The concept of self-esteem has grown from a fragile idea used to ground the newly emerging discipline of psychology to a basic truth about human experience and motivation. Since it first entered the discourse of human sciences in the nineteenth century, self-esteem has become one of the most important concepts in psychological research, psychotherapy, and popular discussions of the self and self-help. High levels of self-esteem are said to lead to a host of positive attributes, such as good academic performance (Dukes & Lorch, 1989), happy marriages (Thornstam, 1992) and a healthy sex life (Hally & Pollack, 1993). In contrast, low levels of self-esteem have been linked to widely varying issues like teenage problems, etc. For some people, low levels of self-esteem are not only a central cause of various psychological problems, but are also an important contributing factor to a multiple of social problems.

Self-esteem is a personality variable that will greatly affect the way a person receives and reacts to a message. Individuals with low self-esteem are generally easier to persuade than those with high self-esteem (Janis & Field, 1959). Persons with low self-esteem are conformists by nature. They have little confidence in their own opinions and are persuaded easily by someone else's ideas. Individuals with high self-esteem have greater confidence in their opinions and find it easier to challenge the ideas of others. This makes them less susceptible to persuasion (Burgoon, Hunsaker & Dawson, 1994).

Self-esteem of the sender and the receiver affects communication. Self-esteem, which is the enduring evaluation of oneself, often determines the confidence in what one is saying and the readiness to accept the views of others. Therefore, in communication process, it is important to use the perception of another person's self-esteem as a means of evaluating certain messages. For example, individuals with high self-esteem may confidently state an opinion even without sufficient evidence, whereas individuals with low self-esteem would hesitate in supporting the unproven viewpoints.

Looking at the general body of research on self-esteem, it is evident that most of the literature deals with global self-esteem, which means the individual's positive or negative attitude toward the self as a totality (Rosenberg, Schooler, Schoenbach & Rosenberg, 1995). Kitano (1989) in a computer search of literature found over 6,500 article titles that explicitly used the term "self-esteem".

Rosenberg Self-Esteem Scale (Rosenberg, 1989) has been used worldwide to measure the global self-esteem, which measures individuals' views of themselves containing both positive and negative components. Rosenberg's scale was originally developed to measure the adolescent's global feeling of self-worth or self-acceptance, and is generally considered the standard against which other measures of self-esteem are compared. The present study investigates the impact of self-esteem on communication styles by using Rosenberg Self-Esteem Scale.

Self-esteem is an intrinsic and universal part of human experience. In fact, the study on self-esteem is so widely done that its role in shaping behaviour has become an undeniable truth about human existence and motivation. The concept of self-esteem has been employed as a tool for unlocking the inherent secrets of human behaviour.

The origin of the concept of self-esteem can be traced to the advent of self-psychology in the late nineteenth and early twentieth century. Within this period, writers like William James, C.H. Cooley, and G. H. Mead, began to position the concept of self at the centre of psychology and social psychology (Coopersmith, 1967). The first reference to self-esteem in psychology can be found in William James' (1950) *Principles of Psychology*. James argued that self-esteem is determined by the ratio of our actualities to our supposed potentialities. During the period, 1940s to the early 1970s, self-esteem became a central concept in experimental and survey studies in psychology and social psychology (Wylie, 1961). In 1965, Rosenberg was the first person to use large-scale survey research techniques to explore the factors, which influence self-esteem. During the period from the late 1960s until the early 1990s, it is observed that the concept of self-esteem was used in self-help and parenting literature. This concept of self-esteem was no longer specialized jargon of psychologists, but a real tool far changing one's life. As the concept of self-esteem became more popular it was considered to be an important aspect of communication behaviour.

Some studies on self-esteem and communication indicate that self-esteem and communication are positively correlated. For example, parent-adolescent communication is positively related to adolescent's self-esteem and inversely related to adolescent loneliness and depression (Brage & Meredith, 1994; Demo, Small & Savin-Williams, 1987; Engar, Howerton & Cobbs, 1993). Huang (1999) investigated the relationship between family communication patterns and set of personality characteristics. Results showed that individuals from conversation-oriented families exhibited greater degree of self-disclosure, desire-for-control, self-esteem and socialibility. Keyton (1999) noted, "when group members communicate directly or indirectly about their relationships with one another, they provide cues about their own and other members' worth and identities, that ultimately affect their self-esteem" (p. 193).

Over the years, several models have been put forth as explanations of how one's self-esteem changes. One can see the important role of interpersonal communication in several of these models, for example, in the need for an accepting relationship between client and therapist in Rogers' (1951) model and for approval from significant others in the research of Bednar, Wells and Peterson (1989) and Harter (1993). Past researches have treated self-esteem either as a social force or as a social product. Rosenberg and Schooler (1989) conducted a study to explore the reciprocal relationships between self-esteem and three problems of youth: juvenile delinquency, poor school performance, and psychological depression. They found that low self-esteem fosters delinquency and that delinquency may enhance self-esteem. These reciprocal effects differ among socio-economic status groups. The relationship between self-esteem and school performance is primarily attributable to the effect of school performance on self-esteem. The causal relationship between self-esteem and depression is bi-directional.

Naturally, communication begins with self (intrapersonal communication) and with others (interpersonal communication). The way we have learned about ourselves as women or as men affects how we communicate with others. It also affects others' perception about us. The way people see us and communicate with us affects our self-esteem and self-esteem affects our communication behaviour.

## Critical Evaluation

Stamp (1999) examined 288 interpersonal research articles published during the past twenty-five years in *Human Communication Research*. Articles published under *Personality Category* focused on the enduring personality characteristics of communicators and how these characteristics affected the communication process. This category included characteristics such as dominance, self-esteem, gender, assertiveness, communication styles, etc. Self-disclosure was another category which examined the level, valence and anticipation of self-disclosure and disclosure as a strategy in interpersonal relationships.

Thus, it is evident that personality characteristics have a great impact on communication styles of individuals. McCallister's (1994) Communication Style Profile Test (CSPT) is a unique test but her observation that sex differences have nothing to do with the communication style does not, however, appear to have been empirically determined. At the same time, the potential impact of gender role orientation on communication style has not been discussed. Keeping these things in mind, the present study proposes to examine the impact of gender role self-perception, self-disclosure and self-esteem on communication style. Through survey of literature, it has been found that in our culture, studies on gender and communication are very rare and perhaps the present work is one of the first to explore the impact of personality characteristics on communication style.

Further, review of literature on gender and communication mentioned in this study indicates that the findings on gender and communication are full of contradictions. Some researches suggest that no substantial sex differences emerge across many aspects of communication behaviours. But the question remains: From where do we derive our attitudes and beliefs about sex differences in communication? To find an answer to this question, the cultural context might be very important in understanding sex differences in communication. Our society is changing rapidly and so is the relationship between women and men. Persons who have been interested in understanding, explaining and predicting communication behaviours between women and men have tried alternative approaches, divergent methods and distinctive philosophies. The present study is an effort to investigate the different communication behaviours based on sex and gender role in our culture by using appropriate method.

The review of literature on self-disclosure shows that the amount of self-disclosure depends on the individual's personality, culture, beliefs and attitudes. The present study investigates the impact of one of the important personality characteristics (i.e., self-disclosure) on communicator style. Snell *et al.* (1986,1988, and 1989) developed a scale named The Masculine and Feminine Self-disclosure Scale (MFSDS). The scale measures the individual's willingness to discuss the instrumental (i.e., masculine) and expressive (i.e., feminine) aspects of themselves with different target groups like male friends, female friends, etc. Snell's scale has been used in this study to see the impact of self-disclosure on McCallister's dominant communication styles. McCallister states that Nobles rarely engage in personal self-disclosure, whereas Reflectives openly engage in it. The study will examine her contention on self-disclosure empirically.

Some researchers have found no difference in the levels of self-esteem of men and women (Drummond, McIntire & Ryan, 1977; E.E. Maccoby & Jacklin, 1974), but there are some who have noted such differences (DeFrancisco & Allison, 1992; Gold, Brush & Sprotzer, 1980; Kimball & Gray, 1982; Steinem, 1992). This inconsistency in findings may be due to developmental differences, different standards, psychological gender, and different types of self-esteem. Steinem (1992) believes that our culture impacts our core self-esteem, and thus, it begins to fluctuate. Change in self-esteem may result in changes in our behaviours including our communication styles. The present study, therefore, would like to examine the impact of self-esteem on communication styles.

Thus, in the light of the above review of literature and discussion, the following hypotheses are proposed:

## Hypotheses

1. Gender role would predict significantly the communication styles.
   (a) Masculine gender role would predict significantly the noble communication style.
   (b) Feminine gender role would predict significantly the reflective communication style.
2. Self-disclosure would predict significantly the communication styles.
3. Self-disclosure with friends as compared to parents would predict significantly the communication styles.
4. Self-esteem would predict significantly the communication styles.
5. Males and females would differ significantly on their communication styles.
6. Communication styles of 'masculine' individuals would differ significantly from those of 'feminine' counterparts.
7. Respondent sex and gender role self-perception would interact to influence the communication styles.
8. Individuals with high masculine self-disclosure would differ significantly from those with low masculine self-disclosure on their communication styles.
9. Individuals with high feminine self-disclosure would differ significantly from those with low feminine self-disclosure on their communication styles.
10. High and low groups of individuals on self-esteem would differ significantly on their communication styles.

# 2

# METHOD

## Sample

The sample consisted of 415 (282 males, 133 females) undergraduate and postgraduate students studying at the Indian Institute of Technology, Kharagpur. These students registered themselves in various courses at different levels in the Autumn Semester, 2000. The Institute is located in the eastern part of the country and is the oldest and the biggest amongst all six IITs. Students get admission in this Institute through all India level admission test.

The students for this study were selected randomly. They represented twenty-three Indian states. Out of total sample, 66 per cent were from urban, 28 per cent were from semi-urban and 6 per cent were from rural background. As high as 82 per cent of the students belonged to nuclear families and the remaining 18 per cent came from joint families. About 50 per cent of the students came from middle-income (between Rs.10,000 and Rs. 20,000) group families, whereas 30 per cent from high-income (above Rs. 20,000) group and 20 per cent from low-income (below Rs. 10,000) group families. Although subjects had different mother languages, English being the medium of instructions in this Institute, was the common language for all. Students, in general, were career-oriented, therefore, quite hard working and of competitive nature. All female students stayed together in the girls' hostel, whereas male students stayed in different boys hostels for undergraduates and postgraduates. Students who served as subjects were unmarried and they had never attended any course related to interpersonal communication. The average age of students was 20.43 years (SD = 2.80) [Table 2.1].

**Table 2.1 :** Sample Characteristics

| *Sex* | *N* | *Age (in yrs.)* | | *Family Type* | | *Home Background* | | |
|---|---|---|---|---|---|---|---|---|
| | | *Mean* | *SD* | *Nuclear* | *Joint* | *Rural* | *Semi-Urban* | *Urban* |
| Males | 282 | 19.58 | 1.78 | 230 | 52 | 19 | 83 | 180 |
| Females | 133 | 22.23 | 3.61 | 110 | 23 | 06 | 35 | 92 |
| **Total** | 415 | 20.43 | 2.80 | 340 | 75 | 25 | 118 | 272 |

## Measures

Data were collected using the following measures:

1. Bem Sex Role Inventory (BSRI)
2. Communication Style Profile Test (CSPT)
3. The Masculine and Feminine Self-Disclosure Scale (MFSDS)
4. Rosenberg Self-Esteem Scale (RSES)

### *Bem Sex Role Inventory (BSRI)*

Bem constructed the Bem Sex Role Inventory (BSRI) in 1974. Since then it has been used worldwide including Japan (Katsurada & Sugihara, 1999; Sugihara & Katsurada, 1999), Malaysia (Ward & Sethi, 1986), and India (Rao & Rao, 1996; Ward & Sethi, 1986). This inventory was designed for conducting empirical research on psychological androgyny. It contained sixty personality characteristics. Twenty of the characteristics were stereotypically feminine (e.g., affectionate, gentle, understanding, sensitive to the needs of others) and twenty were stereotypically masculine (e.g., ambitious, self-reliant, independent, assertive). The BSRI also contained twenty neutral items (e.g., truthful, happy, conceited). This test provided independent assessment of masculinity and femininity through self-reported possession of socially desirable, stereotypically masculine and feminine personality traits. Bem did not view femininity and masculinity at opposite poles of a continuum. In other words, if a person was high in masculine traits, he/she was not necessarily low in feminine traits. The 'androgynous' person was high in both masculine and feminine traits and an individual low in both masculine and feminine traits was called 'undifferentiated'. High on masculinity and low on femininity was called 'masculine' and high on femininity and low on masculinity was called 'feminine' (Fig. 2.1).

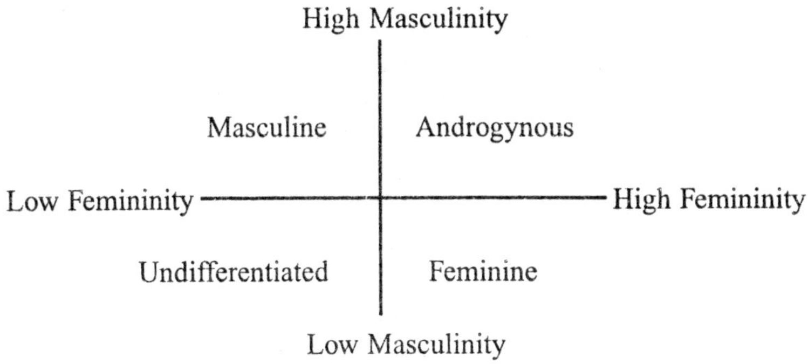


**Fig. 2.1 :** Gender Role Type Based on BSRI

[*Source*: Pearson, West and Turner (1995, p. 62)]

The BSRI is based on a conception of the traditionally sex-typed person as someone who is highly attuned to cultural definitions of sex appropriate behaviours and who uses such definitions as the ideal standard against which his/her own behaviour is to be evaluated. In this way, the traditionally sex-typed person is motivated to help his or her behaviour consistent with an idealized image of femininity or masculinity. In BSRI, items were selected as feminine or masculine based on cultural definitions of sex-typed social desirability. Historically and cross-culturally, femininity and masculinity have represented complementary domains of positive traits and behaviours. According to Parsons and Bales (1955), femininity has been associated with an expressive orientation, an affective concern for the welfare of others and the harmony of the group, whereas masculinity has been associated with an instrumental orientation, a cognitive focus on getting the job done or the problem solved. Similarly, Bakan (1966) has suggested that femininity is associated with "communal" orientation, a concern for the relationship between oneself and others, whereas masculinity is associated with an "agentic" orientation, a concern for oneself as an individual. Finally, Erikson's (1964) anatomical distinction between "inner" (female) and "outer" (male) space represents an analogue to a quite similar psychological distinction between a more "ethical" feminine commitment to "resourcefulness in peacekeeping and devotion in healing" and a masculine "fondness for what works and for what man can make, whether it helps to build or to destroy".

As a preliminary to the item selection for the masculinity and femininity scales, a list of approximately 200 personality characteristics was compiled by Bem and her several students that seemed to be positive in value and either masculine and feminine in tone. This list served as the pool from which the feminine and masculine characteristics were ultimately chosen. A personality characteristic was defined as masculine or feminine if it was judged to be significantly more desirable for one sex than for the other. The test-retest reliabilities for original BSRI (60 items) masculinity and femininity scores were .76 and .89 respectively.

Research has demonstrated that the BSRI is useful (Bem, 1975) and valid (Bem, 1977; Bem, Martyna & Watson, 1976; Holt & Ellis, 1998) for exploring sex role based upon an individual's self-description in terms of society's definitions of differentially desirable traits in American males and females. Culture defines gender roles. In all cultures, biological sex is not the only factor to define being male or being female. Societal values and expectations perpetuate gender role stereotype in a culture, and mandate males to be "masculine" and females to be "feminine". Stereotypes of gender roles created by a culture govern our way of life throughout our existence. These stereotypes vary among different cultures as well as among different ethnic groups (Franklin, 1984; Harris, 1994; Landrine, 1985). Although the BSRI is an established instrument, when this is used outside the United States, it is essential to examine its applicability because gender roles are both biologically and culturally defined (Block, 1973). Sethi and Allen (1996) using BSRI in a cross-cultural study between India and the United States write, "there is considerable overlap between traits considered related to gender in the American and Indian samples. Differences between the countries never reversed stereotypes, but did move items from the gender-related to neutral category. Nearly half of the original BSRI's masculine and feminine items did not reveal significant gender differences in India. The largest agreement across countries was with respect to Bem's neutral items.

Thus, in both the countries a number of traits are considered more desirable for the same gender" (p. 105). Sethi and Allen (1996) collected data from northern India and they admitted that generalization of the results might be questionable, especially in view of the tremendous diversity in India of language, religion and customs. They further suggested that this type of research was needed in other parts of India to clarify the sex roles, as they exist today. In the present study, original BSRI (Bem, 1974, 1981) was used to measure the masculinity and femininity in our culture. In her research, Bem strongly recommended to use the original sixty-item inventory (Bem, 1981). The Inventory consisted of twenty items each reflecting the masculinity and femininity. Twenty filler items were also used, but they were not scored. They served the purpose to know the individual's general tendency to respond in a socially desirable manner. The respondents were asked to indicate how true of them each of the characteristics was on a scale ranging from "always or almost always true" (5) to "never or almost never true" (1).

After the data were collected, a reliability analysis (alpha) was done and alpha coefficient was found to be high. Further, factor analysis was done to check the validity of the test. Many researchers acknowledge the prominent role that factor analysis can play in efforts to establish construct validity (Thompson & Daniel, 1996). For example, Nunnally (1978) noted that historically, "construct validity has been spoken of as [both] trait validity and factorial validity" (p. 111). Similarly, Gorsuch (1983) noted "a prime use of factor analysis has been in the development of both the operational constructs for an area and the operational representatives for the theoretical constructs" (p. 350). In short, "factor analysis is intimately involved with questions of validity...Factor analysis is at the heart of measurement of psychological constructs" (Nunnally, 1978, pp. 112-13).

The forty items measuring masculinity and femininity were factor analysed using the Principle Component Method with Varimax Rotation. The determination of eigenvalue was ensured (set at 2.0) using the screeplot of the items evolved after the initial statistics. The 40 × 40 inter-correlation matrix produced three factors (Factor 1: eigenvalue 5.55, variance accounted for 13.9 per cent; Factor 2: eigenvalue 4.35, variance accounted for 10.9 per cent; Factor 3: eigenvalue 2.32, variance accounted for 5.8 per cent). Items that were not loaded highly (i.e., less than .40) on any of these factors were deleted. However, item Nos. 35 and 38 although not loading highly were retained and item No. 31 loading highly was deleted to make the number of items equal on both the subscales (*Appendix-A*).

Finally, the procedure yielded fifteen items each for masculinity and femininity which were used for the final study. For each respondent, masculinity (M = 50.02, SD = 7.56, alpha = .79) and femininity (M = 56.18, SD = 6.49, alpha = .78) scores were computed by summing the scores (Table 2.3). As recommended by Bem (1981), the subjects were classified on the basis of a median split into four distinct sex role groups: masculine, feminine, androgynous, and undifferentiated. Median on masculinity scale was 50.00 and on femininity scale was 57.00. This sex role groups produced the following distribution (Table 2.2).

**Table 2.2 :** Gender Role Classification: Median Split Method

| | Masculine | | Feminine | | Androgynous | | Undifferentiated | |
|---|---|---|---|---|---|---|---|---|
| Sex | N | Percentage | N | Percentage | N | Percentage | N | Percentage |
| Males | 81 | 28.7 | 50 | 17.7 | 69 | 24.5 | 82 | 29.1 |
| Females | 15 | 11.3 | 62 | 46.6 | 27 | 20.3 | 29 | 21.8 |

## *Communication Style Profile Test (CSPT)*

Respondents completed the Communication Style Profile Test (CSPT, McCallister, 1994) which consisted of sixty items. CSPT was used to assess the three predominant communication styles (a) Noble, (b) Socratic and (c) Reflective that people may employ when interacting with others in both interpersonal and group settings. The items were arranged randomly and each style included twenty items. The respondents were asked to report the way they actually communicated on a scale ranging from "almost always" (5) to "almost never" (1).

Based on reliability analysis (alpha) four items from each sub-scales, i.e., Noble, Socratic and Reflective were deleted, as these items indicated very poor correlation with the total. It was found that upon deletion of the items, alpha coefficient of the sub-scales increased. Later, the selected forty-eight items were factor analysed using the Principle Component Method with Varimax Rotation. The determination of eigenvalue was ensured (set at 2.0) using the screeplot of the items evolved after the initial statistics. The 48 × 48 intercorrelation matrix produced four factors (Factor 1: eigenvalue 4.23, variance accounted for 8.8 per cent; Factor 2: eigenvalue 3.45, variance accounted for 7.2 per cent; Factor 3: eigenvalue 2.89, variance accounted for 6.0 per cent; Factor 4: eigenvalue 2.15, variance accounted for 4.5 per cent). Items that were not loaded highly (i.e., less than .40) on any of these factors were deleted. However, item Nos. 4 and 28 although not loading highly were retained and item Nos. 3 and 54 loading highly were deleted to make the number of items equal on all the three subscales (*Appendix-B*). This procedure yielded thirty items for final study that explored the several aspects of the communication process like competence, willingness, and apprehension about communication.

The Noble communication style is defined as involving assertiveness, directness, domination, impatience and precision. Individuals who prefer this style are characterized as result oriented, bottom line, and who gives his/her opinions on issues openly, but get frustrated when others do not accept the same communication premise. Ten items were used to operationalize this concept including, for example, "I say what I think, and I expect the other person to do the same," "I will interrupt a person who is talking too much" and "If I observe an irritating habit, I tend to tell the other person about it."

The Socratic style is defined as being concerned with rhetoric, the analysis of details, debate and evaluative judgment. Individuals who prefer this style are characterized as argumentative, philosophical, verbose, persuasive and redundant. Ten items were used to operationalize this concept including "I have an excellent ability to recall details, I think words are very important, and I enjoy using them", and "I tend to explain things by using anecdotal stories and hypothetical examples."

The Reflective communication style is defined as being accommodating, non-assertive and showing concern for others. Individuals who demonstrate the reflective style of communication tend to be warm, supportive, patient, soft-spoken, and good listeners. Ten items were used to operationalize this concept including, for example, "I am polite, supportive, and warm when I talk," "I have very good ideas, but my suggestions are often ignored," and "I often feel frustrated because I don't actually say what I really feel."

In a manner suggested by McCallister the three communication style scores were computed by adding the ten items for each communication style for each respondent. The Noble (M = 34.79, SD = 3.99, alpha = .55), the Socratic (M = 33.07, SD = 5.13, alpha = .69) and the Reflective (M = 32.83, SD = 4.47, alpha = .65) indices were used in subsequent analysis (Table 2.3).

**Table 2.3 :** Number of Items, Mean, SD, and Reliability of Variables

| Constructs | Variables | | No of items | Mean of total items | SD | Correlation of each item score with total item score: Minimum | Correlation of each item score with total item score: Maximum | Cronbach's alpha |
|---|---|---|---|---|---|---|---|---|
| Communication Style | Noble | | 10 | 34.79 | 3.99 | .32** | .54** | .55 |
| | Socratic | | 10 | 33.07 | 5.13 | .38** | .61** | .69 |
| | Reflective | | 10 | 32.83 | 4.47 | .41** | .59** | .65 |
| Sex Role | Masculine | | 15 | 50.02 | 7.56 | .34** | .70** | .79 |
| | Feminine | | 15 | 56.18 | 6.49 | .19** | .66** | .78 |
| Self-Disclosure | Masculine | Male Friend | 15 | 50.34 | 11.84 | .59** | .73** | .91 |
| | | Female Friend | 15 | 46.70 | 13.15 | .59** | .77** | .92 |
| | | Father | 15 | 49.85 | 12.27 | .58** | .74** | .91 |
| | | Mother | 15 | 52.18 | 12.58 | .58** | .76** | .91 |
| | Feminine | Male Friend | 15 | 48.49 | 12.11 | .51** | .77** | .91 |
| | | Female Friend | 15 | 47.67 | 13.48 | .43** | .79** | .93 |
| | | Father | 15 | 47.73 | 13.52 | .53** | .80** | .93 |
| | | Mother | 15 | 52.86 | 13.39 | .55** | .80** | .92 |
| Self-Esteem | Self-Esteem | | 10 | 35.31 | 6.28 | .31** | .75** | .82 |

** $p < .001$

The intercorrelation of communication styles was also computed. All correlations were weak. However, between the Noble and Socratic styles ($r = 0.30, p < .001$) a significant positive relationship was seen. A significant negative relationship between the Noble and Reflective style ($r = - 0.09, p < .05$) also emerged. The correlation between the Socratic and Reflective styles ($r = .01, p = .77$) was non-significant.

### *The Masculine and Feminine Self-Disclosure Scale (MFSDS)*

Snell, Belk, and Hawkins (1986); Snell, Belk, Flowers, and Warren (1988); and Snell (1989) used the Masculine and Feminine Self-Disclosure Scale (MFSDS) to test the self-disclosure level of the respondent with target groups like male friends, female friends, etc. The scale consisted of 42 items but only 30 items were taken and twelve filler items were dropped to reduce the length of the questionnaire. Slight modification was done in the language of instructions and in the language of the items to make them easy to understand. Fifteen masculine and fifteen feminine items were used randomly. Some of the items were changed or modified to accommodate cultural suitability, for example, "how often you kiss or hug your family members", and "how often you hold hands with someone". Disclosure to target groups like male friend and female friend was retained, but male clinician and female clinician was replaced by father and mother as most of the respondents in our culture have more discussion with their parents than male/female clinician. The scale measured individual's willingness to discuss the instrumental (e.g., masculine) and expressive (e.g., feminine) aspects of themselves with different target groups: male friend, female friend, father and mother. The respondents were asked to report to what extent they would like to discuss about these (masculine and feminine) items with their male friend, female friend, father, and mother on a scale ranging from "almost always" (5) to "almost never" (1). The items related to masculine disclosure included strong beliefs, self-reliance, assertiveness, leadership abilities and competitiveness. The feminine disclosure items included shyness, tenderness, gentleness, kindness and being warm. The scores on each sub-scale were averaged. The indices of masculine self-disclosure with male friend ($M = 50.34$, $SD = 11.84$, alpha = .91), female friend ($M = 46.70$, $SD=13.15$, alpha = .92), father ($M = 49.85$, $SD=12.27$, alpha = .91), mother ($M = 52.18$, $SD = 12.58$, alpha = .91) and feminine self-disclosure with male friend ($M = 48.49$, $SD = 12.11$, alpha = .91), female friend ($M = 47.67$, $SD = 13.48$, alpha= .93), father ($M = 47.73$, $SD = 13.52$, alpha = .93), mother ($M = 52.86$, $SD =13.39$, alpha = .92) were used in subsequent analysis (Table 2.3). The higher scores correspond to greater willingness to self-disclosure about that aspect of the self. The reliability analysis (alpha) ensured that the test is highly reliable.

To check the factorial validity of the test factor analysis was done. Total number of masculine and feminine self-disclosure items along with four target disclosure groups, (male friend, female friend, father, mother) were 120. It was not possible to do the factor analysis using Varimax Rotation with all these items, as Varimax failed to rotate so many items at a time. Therefore, the masculine and feminine items along with their target groups were analysed separately. The selected 60×60 items of masculine self-disclosure were factor analysed using the Principle Component Method with Varimax Rotation. The determination of eigenvalue was ensured (set at 2.0) using the screeplot of the items evolved after the initial statistics. The 60×60 inter-correlation matrix produced five factors (Factor 1: eigenvalue 16.56, variance accounted for 27.6 per cent; Factor 2: eigenvalue 6.07, variance accounted for 10.1 per cent; Factor 3: eigenvalue 4.0, variance accounted for 6.6 per cent; Factor 4: eigenvalue 2.45, variance accounted for 4.1 per cent; Factor 5: eigenvalue 2.13, variance accounted for 3.6 per cent). It was found that all the items loaded highly on these factors, so none of the items were deleted [*Appendix-C (I)*]. Similarly, the 60×60 intercorrelation matrix for feminine items produced five factors. (Factor 1: eigenvalue 19.60, variance accounted for 32.7 per cent; Factor 2: eigenvalue 5.23, variance accounted for 8.7 per cent; Factor 3: eigenvalue 4.15, variance accounted for 6.9 per cent; Factor 4: eigenvalue 2.58, variance accounted for 4.3 per cent; Factor 5: eigenvalue 2.08, variance accounted for 3.5 per cent). As all the items loaded highly (.40 and above) on these factors, none of the items were deleted [*Appendix-C (II)*].

### *Rosenberg Self-Esteem Scale (RSES)*

Among the most popular and well-utilized measures of self-esteem is the Rosenberg Self-Esteem Scale (Rosenberg, 1989). Rosenberg's scale was originally developed to measure adolescent's global feelings of self-worth or self-acceptance, and is generally considered the standard against which other measures of self-esteem are compared. It included ten items which were scored on a five-point scale ranging from "agree very much" (5) to "disagree very much" (1).

The original sample for which the scale was developed consisted of 5,025 high school juniors and seniors from ten randomly selected schools in New York State. The ten items were presented to the respondent with instructions that they should show their level of agreement on each item on a five-point scale. Out of ten, five items indicated the negative attitudes and the other five positive attitudes. The scores of the negative items were reversed so that in each case the scores go from less to more self-esteem. Some of the items, which reflects the positive attitudes, included, "I take a positive attitude towards myself", and "On the whole, I am satisfied with myself". Items which included the negative attitudes were, "At times I think I am no good at all", and "I certainly feel useless at times."

Thus, the scale is quite well known and used worldwide. It deals with individual's positive or negative attitude towards the self as a totality. The reliability and the validity of the Rosenberg self-esteem scale were tested. The scores of ten items were added for each respondent to find out an index of self-esteem. The result indicated (M = 35.31, SD = 6.28, alpha = .82) which was used in further analysis (Table 2.3). Higher score indicated greater self-esteem. All the ten items of Rosenberg Self-Esteem Scale were also factor analysed using the Principle Component Method with Varimax Rotation. The eigenvalue was set at one. The determination of eigenvalue was ensured using the screeplot of the items evolved after the initial statistics. The $10 \times 10$ intercorrelation matrix produced two factors. (Factor 1: eigenvalue 4.0, variance accounted for 39.8 per cent; Factor 2: eigenvalue 1.04, variance accounted for 10.3 per cent). All the items loaded highly (.40 and above) on these factors, so none of the items were deleted and they all were used for final study (*Appendix-D*).

### *Pilot Study*

A pilot study on 70 subjects was conducted before final data collection. The respondents' scores were carefully examined and the mean values were obtained. The mean scores regarding all the sub-scales were used for statistical analysis. The responses of the tests used in this study were encouraging and gave some ideas about the nature and suitability of the tests. Problems faced by students in filling up the questionnaires were noted down and accordingly were incorporated in the final data collection.

### Test Administration

A set of questionnaires consisting of four parts was administered to subjects. The beginning of the questionnaire contained a paragraph in which the respondents were requested to give their responses as per instructions. They were advised to give their opinion frankly as there was no right or wrong answer for any of the items. They were assured that the views expressed by them will be used exclusively for academic purposes. They were also asked to give some general information about themselves. This information included the name of the respondents, sex, age, roll number, department/centre, name of the state they came from, name of the course they were registered, the type of family they came from, their home background and monthly income of their families. These demographic data were intended to provide the details of sample characteristics (*Appendix-E*).

The title of the test was not mentioned in the questionnaires to avoid bias. The data from the male students were collected in the classroom. About fifty to sixty minutes was required to complete all the questionnaires. The teachers of classes, in which data were to be collected, were requested in advance, so that they made their classes available for this purpose. The questionnaires were in English. All students understood English well but even then, if there were any query regarding any of the items, it was clarified immediately in the class by the researcher. Students were instructed not to discuss about any of the items among themselves and they should give their opinions what actually they feel.

As the number of female students in each class was very small, data had to be collected from their hostel where all the girl students stay together. For this purpose, warden of the girls' hostel was requested and time was fixed to collect the data in a group of ten to twenty girl students at a time. The author of this thesis was present on the spot and if there was any query regarding any of the items, it was clarified immediately. They were also requested to express their views frankly what they really think and were requested not to discuss about any of the items among themselves.

After collecting the data from male and female students, scoring was done within a couple of days. It was found that seventeen questionnaires were incomplete, therefore, they were rejected. Thus, the scores of 415 (males = 282, females = 133) subjects were obtained for further statistical analysis.

# 3

# RESULTS

The present study was designed to assess the impact of gender role self-perception, self-disclosure, and self-esteem on communication style. For this purpose, four measures were used, namely Bem Sex Role Inventory (BSRI), Communication Style Profile Test (CSPT), the Masculine and Feminine Self-Disclosure Scale (MFSDS) and Rosenberg Self-Esteem Scale (RSES). By using suitable statistics, the impacts of gender role self-perception, self-disclosure and self-esteem were examined on three predominant communication styles (i.e., Noble, Socratic, Reflective). Data were analysed using SPSS. Mainly, two forms of analyses have been employed to test the hypotheses:

1. Regression analysis
2. Evaluation of group differences and interactions

The indices of descriptive analysis are provided along with each statistical analysis. The descriptive analysis examines and describes the nature, characteristics and properties of scores obtained through data collection. This includes mean scores and standard deviations for variables consisting of gender role type (masculine, feminine, androgynous, undifferentiated), self-disclosure (masculine, feminine), self-esteem, and communication styles (Noble, Socratic, Reflective).

## Regression Analysis

Regression analysis is supposed to be the most appropriate method to predict one variable from other. In the present study, the stepwise regression analysis was employed to test how far the dependent variables (Noble, Socratic, Reflective) may be predicted from independent variables (Gender Role, Masculine and Feminine Self-Disclosure, and Self-Esteem). The hypotheses and details of stepwise regression analyses have been given below:

### *Hypothesis 1, 2, and 4*

It was hypothesized that gender role would predict significantly the communication styles.

1. (a) Masculine gender role would predict significantly the noble communication style.
   (b) Feminine gender role would predict significantly the reflective communication style.
2. Self-disclosure would predict significantly the communication styles.
3. Self-esteem would predict significantly the communication styles.

The stepwise regression analysis confirmed all the above-mentioned hypotheses. Masculine sex role and feminine self-disclosure explained 12 per cent of the variance ($F = 28.15$, $p < .001$) of noble communication style. Masculine sex role and masculine self-disclosure explained 9 per cent of the variance ($F = 20.72$, $p < .001$) of socratic communication style. Self-esteem, masculine sex role, and feminine sex role explained 21 per cent of the variance ($F = 35.83$, $p < .001$) of reflective communication style.

The standardized β coefficients indicated that individuals with 'masculine' sex role preferred noble communication style and individuals with 'feminine' sex role preferred reflective communication style. Individuals having more masculine self-disclosure showed preference for socratic communication style, and those individuals who had more feminine self-disclosure preferred noble communication style. Self-esteem predicted reflective communication style. Thus, the above-mentioned hypotheses are fully substantiated. Details of stepwise regression analysis are given in Table 3.1.

### *Hypothesis 3*

It was hypothesized that self-disclosure with friends as compared to parents would predict significantly the communication styles. To test this hypothesis regression analysis was conducted. All target groups of masculine and feminine self-disclosure (i.e., male friend, female friend, father, mother) were tested on each communication style. The

**Table 3.1** : Summary of Stepwise Multiple Regression Analysis for Independent Variables Predicting Communication Styles

| Independent Variables→ | Masculine Sex Role | | | Feminine Sex Role | | | Masculine Self-Disclosure | | | Feminine Self-Disclosure | | | Self-Esteem | | | $R^2$ | F |
|---|---|---|---|---|---|---|---|---|---|---|---|---|---|---|---|---|---|
| Dependent Variables↓ | β | SEB | Beta | β | SEB | Beta | β | SEB | Beta | β | SEB | Beta | β | SEB | Beta | | |
| Noble | .16 | .02 | .30** (6.40) | — | — | — | — | — | — | .01 | .004 | .12* (2.56) | — | — | — | .12 | 28.15** |
| Socratic | .16 | .03 | .24** (4.78) | — | — | — | .01 | .006 | .12* (2.43) | — | — | — | — | — | — | .09 | 20.72** |
| Reflective | -.10 | .02 | -.18* (-3.80) | .23 | .03 | .34** (7.79) | — | — | — | — | — | — | -.14 | .03 | -.20** (-4.23) | .21 | 35.83** |

* p < .01
** p < .001

*Note* : t-values of **Beta** are given in parentheses.
β = Unstandardized, **SEB** = Standardized Error of Beta, **Beta** = Standardized Beta Coefficient.

stepwise regression analysis revealed that masculine self-disclosure with male friend explained 6 per cent of the variance of noble communication style ($F = 27.19$, $p < .001$). The masculine and feminine self-disclosure with male friend explained 4 per cent of the variance of reflective communication style ($F = 8.80$, $p < .001$). The standardized β coefficients indicated that those who had more masculine self-disclosure with male friend tended to have noble communication style. Individuals with more feminine self-disclosure with male friend tended to have reflective communication style. Masculine and feminine self-disclosure with other target groups (i.e., female friend, father and mother did not predict significantly communication styles. Details of stepwise regression analysis for masculine and feminine self-disclosure with male friend are given in Table 3.2.

**Table 3.2 :** Summary of Stepwise Multiple Regression Analysis for Masculine and Feminine Self-Disclosure with Male Friend Predicting Communication Styles

| Independent Variables → | Masculine Self-Disclosure with Male Friend | | | Feminine Self-Disclosure with Male Friend | | | $R^2$ | F |
|---|---|---|---|---|---|---|---|---|
| Dependent Variables ↓ | β | SEB | Beta | β | SEB | Beta | | |
| Noble | .08 | .01 | *.24 (5.22) | — | — | — | .06 | *27.19 |
| Socratic | .08 | .02 | *.20 (4.27) | — | — | — | .04 | *18.28 |
| Reflective | -.11 | .03 | *-.29 (-3.51) | .13 | .03 | *.36 (4.19) | .04 | *8.80 |

*p <.001

*Note*: t- values of Beta are given in parentheses.

## Evaluation of Group Differences and Interactions

Using appropriate statistics, group differences and interactions for hypotheses were tested. Descriptive analysis of data and other statistical details for each hypothesis are given below:

## *Hypothesis 5, 6 and 7*

It was hypothesised that:

5. Males and females would differ significantly on their communication styles.
6. Communication styles of 'masculine' individuals would differ significantly from those of 'feminine' individuals.
7. Respondent sex and gender role self-perception would interact to influence the communication styles.

Tables (3.3 to 3.5) and Figures (3.1 to 3.3) give the descriptive analysis of the data for the above-mentioned hypotheses. Table 3.3 and Figure 3.1 show the descriptive data for sex and communication styles, Table 3.4 and Figure 3.2 describe data for gender role self-perception and communication styles. Table 3.5 and Figure 3.3 describe interactions of sex by gender role and communication styles.

**Table 3.3 :** Mean with SD of Males and Females on Communication Styles as Dependent Measure

| Sex → Communication Styles ↓ | Male (N=282) | Female (N=133) |
|---|---|---|
| Noble | 35.06<br>(3.96) | 34.23<br>(4.04) |
| Socratic | 33.29<br>(5.10) | 32.60<br>(5.19) |
| Reflective | 33.27<br>(4.36) | 31.89<br>(4.56) |

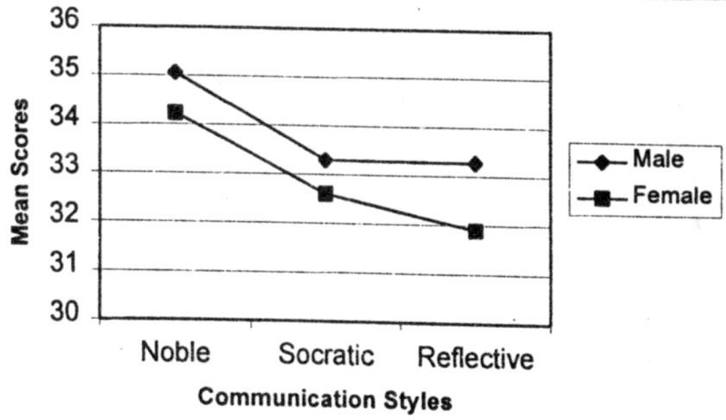


**Fig. 3.1 :** Mean Scores of Males and Females on Communication Styles

**Table 3.4 : Mean with SD of Gender Role Type on Communication Styles as Dependent Measure**

| Gender Role Type → Communication Styles ↓ | Masculine (N=96) | Feminine (N=112) | Androgynous (N=96) | Undifferentiated (N=111) |
|---|---|---|---|---|
| Noble | 36.46 (3.58) | 34.05 (4.08) | 35.28 (3.62) | 33.68 (4.07) |
| Socratic | 34.16 (4.99) | 32.45 (4.98) | 34.45 (5.05) | 31.57 (5.02) |
| Reflective | 30.55 (4.42) | 34.44 (4.35) | 33.42 (4.29) | 32.67 (3.96) |

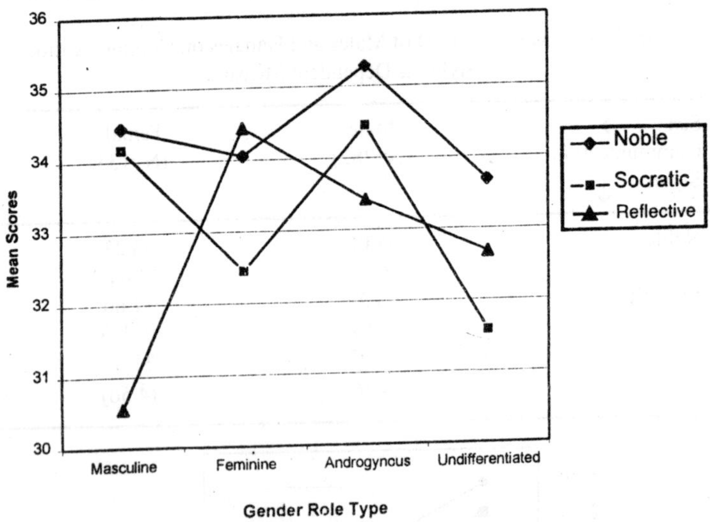


**Fig. 3.2 : Mean Scores of Gender Role Type on Communication Styles**

**Table 3.5 :** Mean with SD of Sex and Gender Role Type on Communication Styles as Dependent Measure

| Gender Role Type → | Masculine | | Feminine | | Androgynous | | Undifferentiated | |
|---|---|---|---|---|---|---|---|---|
| Sex → Communication Styles ↓ | Male (N=81) | Female (N=15) | Male (N=50) | Female (N=62) | Male (N=69) | Female (N=27) | Male (N=82) | Female (N=29) |
| Noble | 36.39 | 36.80 | 34.48 | 33.70 | 35.55 | 34.59 | 33.67 | 33.69 |
| | (3.67) | (3.16) | (3.74) | (4.32) | (3.78) | (3.14) | (4.05) | (4.18) |
| Socratic | 34.35 | 33.13 | 32.74 | 32.21 | 34.88 | 33.33 | 31.24 | 32.48 |
| | (4.79) | (6.08) | (5.03) | (4.97) | (5.41) | (3.84) | (4.48) | (6.32) |
| Reflective | 30.82 | 29.07 | 35.84 | 33.31 | 34.16 | 31.52 | 33.36 | 30.69 |
| | (4.48) | (3.84) | (4.04) | (4.29) | (4.07) | (4.33) | (3.40) | (4.76) |

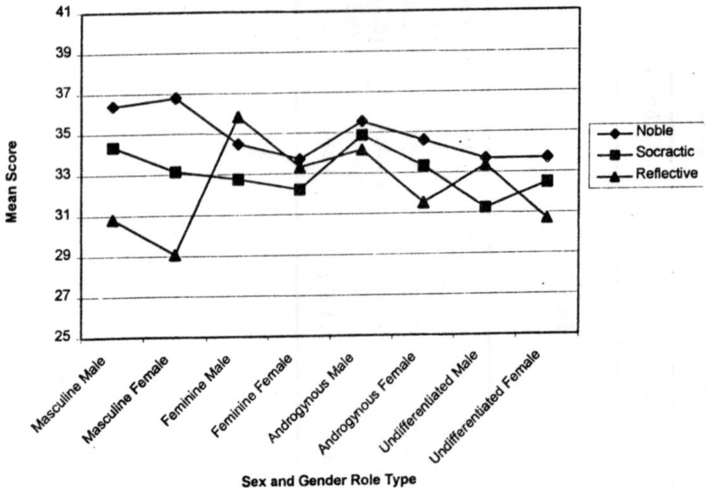


**Fig. 3.3 :** Mean Scores of Sex and Gender Role Type on Communication Styles

The three dependent measures (noble, socratic, and reflective communication styles) were analysed by using the univariate tests. A 2×4 factorial design was employed with respondent sex (male, female) and gender role type (masculine, feminine, androgynous, undifferentiated) as independent measures.

The hypothesis that males would differ significantly from females on their communication styles was tested. The univariate tests showed significant 'sex' main effects on noble ($F = 4.10$, $df = 1,407$, $p = .044$) and reflective ($F = 10.03$, $df = 1,407$, $p = .002$) communication style measures. However, 'sex' main effect for the socratic measure was not significant ($F = 1.71$, $df = 1,407$, $p = .192$). Thus, the above-mentioned hypothesis is partially supported.

Examination of mean scores associated with respondent sex on communication styles as dependent measure revealed that males ($M = 35.06$) scored higher on noble communication style than did females ($M = 34.23$). For the reflective communication style also, males scored higher ($M = 33.27$) than females ($M = 31.89$) (Table 3.3). The statistical details are given in Table 3.6.

**Table 3.6** : Univariate F-Tests: Effect of Sex on Communication Styles

| Variables | SS | MS | F | p |
|---|---|---|---|---|
| Noble | 61.31 | 61.31 | *4.10 | .044 |
| Socratic | 42.94 | 42.94 | 1.71 | .192 |
| Reflective | 170.81 | 170.81 | *10.03 | .002 |

* Significant

Univariate tests of the gender role were significant (p < .001) across all three communication style measures [Noble (F = 9.85, df = 3,407), Socratic (F = 7.44, df = 3,407) and Reflective (F = 22.51, df = 3,407)]. Details of statistical analysis are given in Table 3.7. Descriptive data for gender role type with communication styles as dependent measure revealed that the 'masculine' group (M = 36.46) had higher score than other gender role groups on the noble communication style. On the other hand, the 'feminine' group (M = 34.44) had higher score on the reflective communication style (Table 3.4). Thus, the hypothesis that communication styles of 'masculine' individuals would differ significantly from those of 'feminine' counterparts is confirmed.

**Table 3.7** : Univariate F-Tests: Communication Styles as a Function of Gender Role

| Variables | SS | MS | F | p |
|---|---|---|---|---|
| Noble | 442.19 | 147.39 | *9.85 | < .001 |
| Socratic | 560.60 | 186.87 | *7.43 | < .001 |
| Reflective | 1150.46 | 383.49 | *22.51 | < .001 |

* Significant

Finally, the sex by gender role type interaction was examined for all three communication styles. The results revealed non-significant interactions (Table 3.8).

As mentioned above, the main effect of gender role self-perception was significant on all three-communication styles. Further analysis was done to see the significant differences between groups. Post-hoc tests (Student-Newman-Keul 't' test, p < .001) were computed for each communication style index (noble, socratic, reflective) across each level of gender role type (masculine, feminine, androgynous,

**Table 3.8** : Univariate F-Tests: Communication Styles as a Function of Sex by Gender Role
(df = 3,407)

| Variables | SS | MS | F | P |
|---|---|---|---|---|
| Noble | 21.76 | 7.25 | .48 | .693 |
| Socratic | 92.04 | 30.68 | 1.22 | .302 |
| Reflective | 7.96 | 2.65 | .16 | .926 |

undifferentiated). Details of post-hoc comparison between gender role types for each communication style are given in Table 3.9.

**Table 3.9 :** Post-hoc Comparison between Gender Role Types for each Communication Style

| Communication Styles ↓ | Gender Role Types ↓→ | Mas-culine | Femi-nine | And-rogynous | Undif-ferentiated |
|---|---|---|---|---|---|
| | Masculine | | * | * | * |
| | Feminine | — | | — | — |
| Noble | Androgynous | — | * | | * |
| | Undifferentiated | — | — | — | |
| | Masculine | | * | — | * |
| | Feminine | — | | — | — |
| Socratic | Androgynous | — | * | | * |
| | Undifferentiated | — | — | — | |
| | Masculine | | — | — | — |
| | Feminine | * | | — | * |
| Reflective | Androgynous | * | — | | — |
| | Undifferentiated | * | — | — | |

*p <.001

### *Hypothesis 8*

It was hypothesized that individuals with high masculine self-disclosure would differ significantly from those with low masculine self-disclosure on their communication styles. High and low groups of masculine self-disclosure based on mean were tested for difference on their communication styles. The results indicated that high and low groups did differ significantly on noble and socratic communication styles. These groups, however, did not differ significantly on reflective communication style. The statistical details are reported in Table 3.10. Descriptive data of high and low groups of masculine self-disclosure (Table 3.10 and Figure 3.4) indicated that individuals who disclosed more about their masculine traits and behaviours tended to have noble communication style (M = 35.62). The comparison of mean scores indicated that reflective communication style was lower than the noble and socratic communication styles. This indicated that those individuals who had a low level of masculine self-disclosure tended to have reflective communication style (M = 32.76).

**Table 3.10 :** Significance of Difference between High and Low Groups of Masculine Self-Disclosure on Communication Styles as Dependent Measure

| Communication Styles | Masculine Self-Disclosure | Mean | SD | N | t | df | p |
|---|---|---|---|---|---|---|---|
| Noble | High | 35.62 | 3.46 | 205 | *4.27 | 413 | <.001 |
| | Low | 33.98 | 4.32 | 210 | | | |
| Socratic | High | 34.16 | 5.26 | 205 | *4.37 | 413 | <.001 |
| | Low | 32.00 | 4.78 | 210 | | | |
| Reflective | High | 32.76 | 4.58 | 205 | -.31 | 413 | .760 |
| | Low | 32.89 | 4.36 | 210 | | | |

* Significant

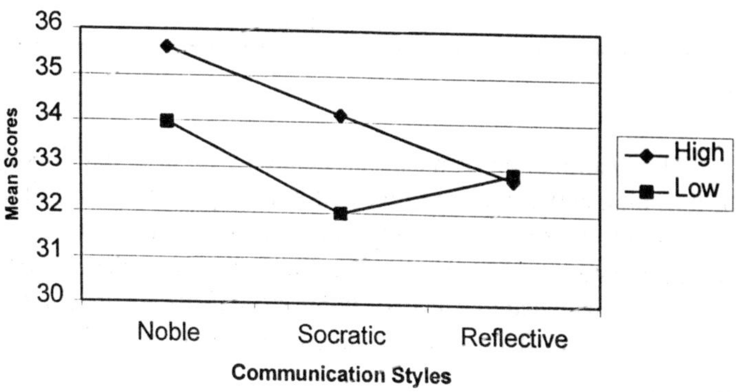


**Fig. 3.4 :** Mean Scores of High and Low Groups of Masculine Self-Disclosure on Communication Styles

### *Hypothesis 9*

It was hypothesized that individuals with high feminine self-disclosure would differ significantly from those with low feminine self-disclosure on their communication styles. High and low groups of feminine self-disclosure were formed on the basis of mean scores. The results indicated that high and low groups differed significantly on noble and socratic communication styles, but failed to differ significantly on reflective communication style. Table 3.11 gives statistical details of high and low groups of feminine self-disclosure with communication styles as the dependent measure.

**Table 3.11 :** Significance of Difference between High and Low Groups of Feminine Self-Disclosure on Communication Styles as Dependent Measure

| Communication Styles | Feminine Self-Disclosure | Mean | SD | N | t | df | p |
|---|---|---|---|---|---|---|---|
| Noble | High | 35.45 | 3.56 | 203 | *3.33 | 413 | < .001 |
| | Low | 34.16 | 4.29 | 212 | | | |
| Socratic | High | 34.11 | 5.20 | 203 | *4.13 | 413 | < .001 |
| | Low | 32.07 | 4.87 | 212 | | | |
| Reflective | High | 33.04 | 4.72 | 203 | .96 | 413 | .337 |
| | Low | 32.62 | 4.20 | 212 | | | |

* Significant

The examination of means associated with high and low groups of feminine self-disclosure revealed that respondents who disclosed more about their feminine traits and behaviours tended to have noble communication style (M = 35.45). Further, it was also evident that individuals who had low level of feminine self-disclosure (M = 33.04) tended to have reflective communication style (Fig. 3.5).

### *Hypothesis 10*

It was hypothesized that high and low groups of individuals on self-

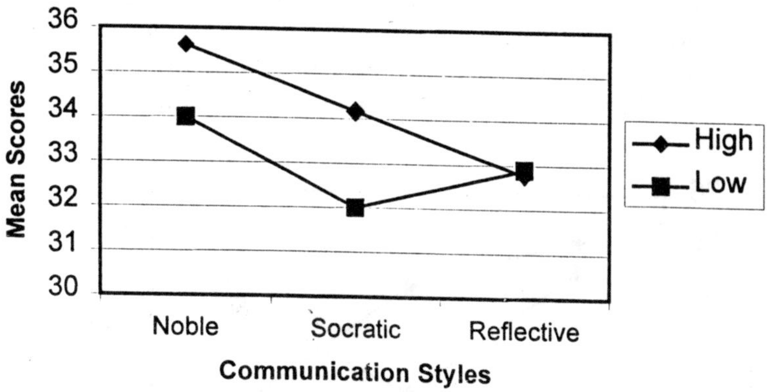


**Fig. 3.5 :** Mean Scores of High and Low Groups of Feminine Self-Disclosure on Communication Styles

esteem would differ significantly on their communication styles. Before testing this hypothesis, the sex difference on self-esteem was examined. The t-test revealed non-significant difference ($t = -.90$, $p = .366$). Later, on the basis of mean scores high and low groups were formed. The analysis revealed that high and low groups of individuals differed significantly on their socratic and reflective communication styles. However, no significant difference was found on noble communication style. The details of statistical analysis are given in Table 3.12 and Figure 3.6.

**Table 3.12 :** Significance of Difference between High and Low Groups of Self-Esteem on Communication Styles as Dependent Measure

| Communication Styles | Self-Esteem | Mean | SD | N | t | df | p |
|---|---|---|---|---|---|---|---|
| Noble | High | 35.12 | 3.96 | 199 | 1.58 | 413 | .114 |
| | Low | 34.49 | 4.01 | 216 | | | |
| Socratic | High | 34.15 | 5.09 | 199 | *4.20 | 413 | <.001 |
| | Low | 32.07 | 4.98 | 216 | | | |
| Reflective | High | 31.80 | 4.37 | 199 | *–4.59 | 413 | <.001 |
| | Low | 33.77 | 4.36 | 216 | | | |

* Significant

Examination of mean scores revealed that individuals with high self-esteem tended to have noble (M = 35.12) than socratic (M = 34.15) communication style. Individuals with low self-esteem tended to have reflective (M = 31.80) communication style (Fig. 3.6).

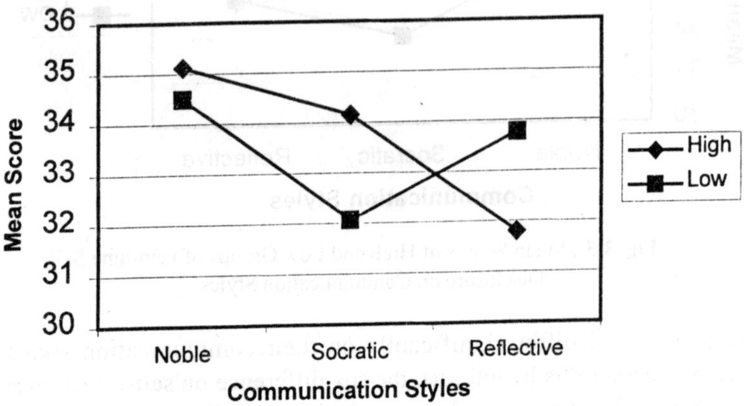


**Fig. 3.6 :** Mean Scores of High and Low Groups of Self-Esteem on Communication Styles

## Summary of Findings

To sum up, the stepwise regression analysis revealed that the personality characteristics (gender role, masculine and feminine self-disclosure and self-esteem) used as independent variables in this study predicted communication styles (i.e., Noble, Socratic, Reflective). Individuals high on masculinity preferred noble communication style, whereas individuals high on femininity showed preference for reflective communication style. Respondents with high masculine self-disclosure intended for socratic and those who had high feminine self-disclosure intended for noble communication style. The impact of self-disclosure with different target groups (i.e., male friend, female friend, father and mother) on communication styles was also tested. The regression analysis revealed that those who had more masculine self-disclosure with male friend tended to have noble communication style while individuals with more feminine self-disclosure with male friend tended to have reflective communication style. Individuals low on their self-esteem indicated preference for reflective communication style.

The univariate tests revealed that males and females differed significantly on noble and reflective communication styles. However, they did not differ on socratic communication style. Examination of mean scores associated with respondent sex on communication styles as dependent measure revealed that males scored high on all three communication styles as compared to females. The gender role self-perception showed significant differences on communication styles. 'Masculine' individuals differed significantly from those of 'feminine' individuals on their communication styles. Mean scores belonging to gender role and communication styles as dependent measure suggested that 'masculine' individuals preferred noble communication style and 'feminine' individuals preferred reflective communication style. The sex by gender role type interaction was also examined. The results revealed non-significant interactions.

High and low groups of masculine self-disclosure differed significantly on noble and socratic communication styles. However, the two groups did not differ on reflective communication style. Mean scores associated with high and low groups of masculine self-disclosure on communication style as dependent measure indicated that individuals who disclosed more about their masculine traits and behaviours tended to have noble and those who disclosed less about their masculine traits and behaviours tended to have reflective communication style.

Similarly, high and low groups of feminine self-disclosure did differ significantly on noble and socratic communication styles, but failed to differ on reflective communication style. Mean scores associated with high and low groups of feminine self-disclosure on communication style as dependent measure indicated that individuals who disclosed more about their feminine traits and behaviours tended to have noble and those who disclosed less about their feminine traits and behaviours tended to have reflective communication style.

Males and females did not differ significantly on their self-esteem, but independent of biological sex, high and low groups of individuals on self-esteem differed significantly on socratic and reflective communication styles. However, these groups did not differ on noble communication style. Examination of mean scores associated with high and low groups of self-esteem and communication style as a dependent measure indicated that individuals with high self-esteem tended to have noble and individuals with low self-esteem preferred reflective communication style.

# 4

# DISCUSSION

In the present study, the impact of gender role self-perception, self-disclosure, and self-esteem has been tested on communication styles. Results of this study are based on regression analysis and evaluation of group differences and interactions. It has been found that all the three independent variables predict communication styles, as defined by Linda McCallister. After testing the predictability of independent variables for dependent variables, the group differences have been examined for each communication style. For the convenience of understanding, findings are discussed below in three parts based on the relationship between independent variables and communication styles.

## I

## GENDER ROLE SELF-PERCEPTION AND COMMUNICATION STYLES

It was hypothesized that gender role would predict the communication styles. Specifically, masculine gender role would predict the noble communication style and feminine gender role would predict the reflective communication style. The regression analysis confirms these hypotheses. It has been found that individuals high on 'masculine' personality traits tend to have noble communication style, whereas those who are high on 'feminine' traits have reflective communication style. Individuals high on 'masculine' traits also predict socratic communication style. However, comparison of the Beta coefficients indicates that 'masculine' individuals have greater preference for noble communication style to any other style. As the present findings are based mainly on the typologies of McCallister's communication styles, it would be appropriate to consider the conceptualization of communication styles by other researchers as well.

The construct of communication style has long been a topic of interest among scholars. Style refers to the way one communicates. Watzlawick, Beavin and Jackson's relational communication model (1967) defines the study of style, which focuses on the message's interpretation by the receiver and its impact on what is being said and how it is being said. Communication style is "the way one verbally, nonverbally, and paraverbally interacts to signal how literal meaning should be taken, interpreted, filtered, or understood" (Norton, 1983, p. 11). According to Tannen (1986), people have different conversational styles, and therefore, when speakers from different parts of the country, or of different ethnic or class backgrounds, talk to each other, it is likely that their words will not be understood exactly as they were meant.

Norton's Communicator Style Scale (1983) examines nine variables: dominant, dramatic, contentious, animated, impression-leaving, relaxed, attentive, open and friendly. A dominant communicator takes charge of the conversation, while a contentious style is more argumentative. A dramatic communicator uses stories, metaphors, exaggerated movements, etc., while an animated style refers to the use of subtle nonverbal cues. A relaxed communicator shows low-tension levels, while an attentive communicator lets others know that he or she is listening. A person who readily reveals information about himself or herself is described as open, and a person who leaves an impact on the receiver's memory has used an impression-leaving style. The friendly style recognizes others positively. Further, Norton (1983) has concluded that these nine components actually reflect a single continuum ranging from non-directive communicative style through directive communicative style. The non-directive style embraces the attentive communicator who encourages, accommodates, and acknowledges others. On the other end of the continuum, the directive style involves the dominant communicator who talks frequently and takes control in social situations (Kirtley & Weaver, 1999).

Following a factor analysis of Norton's (1978) original inventory, Hansford and Hatti (1987) have found an underlying structure defined by an attentive/supportive dimension and a dominant/animated dimension that parallel the non-directive and directive communication styles. The well developed tool for exploring variations in the way people perceive themselves interacting with others is the Communication Style Profile Test (CSPT) by McCallister (1994). McCallister's conceptualization of communication style, which appears to have evolved from the earlier work of Norton (1978), and Hart, Carlson, and Eadie (1980), involves three (rather than two) predominant styles. These are Noble, Socratic and Reflective.

It was hypothesized that communication styles reported by males would differ significantly from those of females. The findings indicate that males and females differ significantly on noble and reflective communication styles, but fail to differ on socratic communication style. It is interesting to note that males as compared to females have scored higher on all three communication styles. However, it has been further observed that both sexes scored high on noble and low on reflective communication style. The present findings, thus, suggest that both males and females prefer noble to other communication styles. These findings are consistent with the findings of other researchers who have found no clear sex differences in communication styles. Montgomery and Norton (1981) report two studies that address the issue of biological sex and communicator style. Both studies use self-report data by students in interpersonal communication classes at Purdue University, USA. In the first study, males and females differed significantly on *precise*, *friendly*, and *animated* dimensions. In the second study, *contentious*, *precise*, and *animated* dimensions were significantly different. Females reported higher scores on the *friendly* and *animated* dimensions; males reported higher means on the *contentious* and *precise* dimensions. Differences, although not significant, were reported on all dimensions. *Dominant*, *precise*, *relaxed*, *attentive* and *animated* had mean differences in the same direction for both studies. Gudykunst and Lim (1985) also used self-report data from college students in communication classes. All dimensions were administered, but four of these dimensions were eliminated due to low reliability. The remaining dimensions, with the exceptions of communicator image, were found to differ significantly. Men reported higher scores on all dimensions studied: dominant, contentious, impression-leaving, relaxed, dramatic, and communicator image.

Heiss (1991), contrary to stereotypic beliefs, has found that males and females display equal power and dominance through their communication styles in intimate relationships. Wheelen and Verdi (1992) report no stereotypic sex differences in the categories of task, maintenance, or verbal participation. Simkins-Bullock and Wildman (1991) state that sex differences do not explain substantial differences in the type of language incorporated in the communication styles of males and females. A meta-analysis conducted by Lustig and Andersen (1990) indicates no sex differences in the communication pattern. Similarly, Hyde and Linn (1988) in a meta-analysis have found no sex differences in verbal ability.

Though researchers have found non-significant differences in the communication styles of males and females, some findings indicate clear differences. For example, Burleson and Samter (1992) have found sex differences to be significant in social participation and communication skills. Fitzpatrick, Mulac and Dindia (1995) report that men with more traditional beliefs and a strong masculine sex-role identity are less likely to modify their gender-preferential speech when conversing with women, whereas women's accommodation is unaffected by their traditionalism or their sex-role identity. Coates (1986), in a review of the literature, notes that women tend to masculinize their speech while talking with males; but conversely, men accommodating to a feminine style, occurs less frequently.

Authors like Aries (1987), Kramarae (1989), Lakoff (1975) and Tannen (1990) argue that men and women differ greatly in the way they communicate and interact with others. Berryman-Fink and Wilcox (1983) opine that females use communication as a socio-emotional function and males use it to fulfil the task or as an instrumental function. Similarly, Kirtley and Weaver (1999) state that females have a socially oriented style of communicating, whereas males have a more straightforward and result-oriented style of communicating. Doyle and Paludi (1991) report the female speech to be indirect, while male speech is considered direct and powerful. Tannen (1990, p. 42) comments, "if women speak and hear a language of connection and intimacy, while men speak and hear a language of status and independence, then communication between men and women can be like cross-cultural communication, prey to a clash of conversational styles. Instead of different dialects, it has been said they speak different *genderlects*". Recent socio-linguistic researches in various cultures have noted sex differences in the speech styles of adults (e.g., Philips,

Steele & Tanz, 1987; Thorne, Kramarae & Henley, 1983). Numerous scholars in the area of gender and communication observe the stereotypical role of male and female. Females have been characterized as emotional, passive, gentle, highly talkative and having an abundance of facial expressions. Males, on the other hand, have been characterized as task-oriented, blunt, aggressive, ambitious and independent (Canary, Emmers-Sommer & Faulkner, 1997; Deaux & Lewis, 1983; Doyle & Paludi, 1991; Hall, 1984; Kramarae, 1989; Lott, 1987; Lindzey & Aronson, 1985; Tannen, 1990). Thus, the literature on gender and communication mentioned in this study indicates that the findings of communication behaviours of males and females are full of contradictions. Future researchers will keep on trying to get an answer to the question: From where do we derive our attitudes and beliefs about sex differences in communication? The present study partially supports McCallister's (1994) observation that sex differences have nothing to do with communication styles. The origin of these sex differences in communication style remains unclear, but one possible explanation may be that these findings have their own cultural biases.

The hypothesis that follows posited that communication styles of 'masculine' individuals would differ significantly from those of 'feminine' individuals. Results have confirmed this hypothesis. The findings based on gender role self-perception and communication styles are consistent with earlier research (e.g., Leaper, 1987; Kirtley & Weaver, 1999; Weaver, Fitch-Hauser, Villaume & Thomas, 1993). The present findings reveal that, independent of biological sex, the 'masculine' individuals report a preference for a goal-oriented, assertive and dominant communication style (i.e., noble communication style). Nobles speak with confidence and authority. Thus, their remarks are usually given serious attention and consideration. They have the potential to be energetic, and to make quick decisions. All these qualities together project them as powerful persons. On the other hand, the 'feminine' individuals report a preference for a supportive, caring, and expressive communication style (i.e., reflective communication style). Reflective communicators are concerned with the human feelings in an interaction. They believe that the communication decorum should be polite and conflict-free. They always try to maintain warm, calm and polite communication decorum, and avoid open conflict by withholding negative opinions and often say what the other person wants to hear rather than what they really feel.

Considering the earlier research (e.g., Berryman-Fink & Wilcox, 1983; Kramer, 1974; Kramarae, 1989; Lakoff, 1975; Simkins-Bullock & Wildman, 1991; Tannen, 1990), the present findings suggest that gender role differences provide a better explanation for variations in communication styles than sex differences. As mentioned earlier, Tannen (1990), Doyle and Paludi (1991), Gray (1992), Hall (1984), Kramer (1974), Kramarae (1989), and Lindzey & Aronson (1985) have argued that females speak and hear a language of negotiating relationships, connection, and rapport, whereas males speak and hear a language of status and independence. Mean scores of masculinity and femininity on Bem Sex Role Inventory used in the present study indicate that individuals scored higher on femininity traits than on masculinity traits. This trend is contradictory to the findings of Kirtley and Weaver (1999), where individuals scored higher on masculinity than femininity traits. This type of result may be due to the cultural differences of the two countries—in the Indian culture, as compared to the American culture, individuals in general tend to have more feminine traits than masculine. On the other hand, people in American culture tend to have more masculine traits than feminine. Thus, gender roles and communication styles need to be understood taking the cultural perspectives into context.

The results of gender role and communication style in the present study are based on the individual's self-perceptions rather than on evaluation of others. It is quite obvious that the criteria we use while forming perceptions of ourselves might be absolutely different from how we perceive others. When we evaluate ourselves, biological sex is generally not a question. But when we encounter other people, their physical and sexual attributes are often the first characteristics we would like to scrutinize. Assessing their gender roles may come much later. When we meet people for the first time, for instance, a first step in assessing their biological sex is to decide what role they can play in our lives (i.e., friend, mate, lover, etc.). A second step is deciding if their gender role orientation is appropriate for our desires, needs, or tastes, which can take more time and effort. Thus, although these things are not really important in self-perceptions, it is the interaction between sex and gender roles that might be critical in how we perceive others.

The findings in this study, however, suggest that these two factors are independent of each other in reporting self-perceptions.

Comparisons between gender role types for each communication style reveal that *masculine* individuals differ from *feminine, androgynous* and *undifferentiated* types, and *androgynous* individuals differ from *feminine*, and *undifferentiated* types on noble communication style. Mean associated with gender role type with communication styles as a dependent measure reveals that *masculine* individuals tend to have noble rather than other communication styles. Further, *masculine* individuals differ from *feminine* and *undifferentiated*, and *androgynous* differ from *feminine* and *undifferentiated* on socratic communication style. Mean scores confirm that *androgynous* prefer socratic to other communication styles. *Feminine* individuals differ from *masculine* and *undifferentiated*, and *androgynous* and *undifferentiated* differ from *masculine* individuals on reflective communication style. Mean scores indicate that *feminine* individuals tend to have reflective rather than other communication styles. Post-hoc comparison confirms that *masculine* respondents have noble and *feminine* respondents have reflective communication style.

That sex and gender role self-perception would interact to influence communication styles is the hypothesis tested next. Results reveal non-significant interaction effect of sex and gender role variables. Consistent with the findings of Kirtley and Weaver (1999), the present findings suggest that there was no interaction between sex and gender role self-perception that could influence the communication styles of the respondents. Thus, it is evident that independent of biological sex, gender role differences give a better explanation for understanding the communication styles of individuals.

## II

## SELF-DISCLOSURE AND COMMUNICATION STYLES

In this part, hypotheses related to self-disclosure have been discussed. First, it was hypothesized that self-disclosure would predict communication styles. It has been found that masculine and feminine self-disclosures do affect communication styles. Individuals with high masculine self-disclosure tend to have socratic, and those with high feminine self-disclosure tend to have noble communication style.

Literature based on self-disclosure shows that the amount of self-disclosure depends on an individual's personality, culture, beliefs and attitudes. Individuals who disclose more about their masculine traits and behaviours tend to have socratic communication style. As proposed by McCallister (1994) socratic communicators enjoy talking. They openly engage in discussion, negotiation, debate and arbitration. They tend to have poor listening habits. All these qualities characterize a socratic communicator as having high masculine self-disclosure. Disclosing more about masculine traits and behaviours means that the individual possesses certain personality characteristics which enable him/her to disclose more about his/her masculine traits and behaviours. A socratic speaks with confidence and from a base of knowledge. Thus, his/her remarks are usually given serious attention and consideration.

Individuals with high feminine self-disclosure have inclination for noble communication style. According to McCallister, Nobles are supposed to be direct, straightforward, frank and spontaneous. This shows that Nobles do not have hesitation to disclose about their personality traits and behaviours to others. Nobles have scored high on their feminine self-disclosure in the present study. The personality characteristics of Nobles as described by McCallister give support for the present finding in Indian culture. The findings of some other researchers in this context have been discussed further.

Self-disclosure has been most widely researched so far as the talking behaviour of individuals is concerned. Researchers assume that revealing intimate information about oneself is healthy. For Jourard (1959), self-disclosure is a prerequisite for a healthy personality, but in real life, people may not have "reasons" like this or may have other reasons, embedded in the conversational realities of everyday life that tend to influence self-disclosing behaviour. Self-disclosure involves individuals conveying information about themselves to others that the other people do not know (Altman & Taylor, 1973). Barnlund's (1975) research in Japan and the United States supports this contention. Culture has also a great impact on self-disclosure. Barnlund (1975) contends that "the greater the cultural homogeneity, the greater the meaning conveyed in a single word, the more that can be implied rather than stated" (p. 162). This implies that explicit self-disclosure is not needed to convey intimate information. Gudykunst, Yoon and

Nishida (1987) found that the greater the degree of collectivism present in a culture, the greater the differences between ingroup (i.e., classmate) and outgroup (i.e., stranger) communication in terms of amount of personalization (e.g., intimacy of communication) and synchronization (i.e., coordination of communication) and of difficulty in communication.

Self-disclosure lies at the heart of the process of interpersonal communication. It gives an important indication by which others know what is going on inside the communicator. Of course, self-disclosure is not always easy. Our natural tendency is to hide feelings of incompetency, loneliness, guilt, worries over love and rejection, conflicts over anger and resentment towards loved ones. Even when the feelings involved are not intense, self-disclosure may still be difficult, because of well-learned habits that help us to avoid emotional hurt. In our society it is observed that people are accustomed to hiding what they really want, think, or feel. This may affect our communication styles. Confiding in others and receiving their confidence is, therefore, one of the most effective interpersonal communication tools (Barker, 1978).

In examining various aspects of self-disclosure, Pearson, West and Turner (1995) have observed a general pattern that women self-disclose more, they are more aware of the cues that affect their self-disclosure. This is because they are socialized to be open and expressive, that is, our culture promotes self-disclosure among women, yet restricts this behaviour among men. Thus, self-disclosure is paramount in the development of our healthy relationships. Self-disclosure appears to be a generally positive communication skill when it is understood and used in moderation.

The basic characteristic of self-disclosure as an interaction is that it occurs in a dyad. The earliest literature on self-disclosure discusses its "dyadic effect". The study by Jourard suggests that self-disclosure occurs only in the dyad and a large number of studies have investigated it in this setting (Winstead, 1986; Zillman, Weaver, Mundorf & Aust, 1986). Researchers who have studied self-disclosure within the dyad have concluded that self-disclosure is generally reciprocal, that is, as the disclosure of one person increases, so does that of the other person (Feigenbaum, 1977).

The present findings indicate that reflective communicators tend to disclose less about their masculine or feminine traits and behaviours.

The low level of disclosure about their masculine and feminine traits and behaviours in reflective communicators seems to be consistent with the personality characteristics as proposed by McCallister (1994). She observes that reflective communicators tend to keep quiet rather than say something that would hurt the other person's feelings. This type of behaviour in reflective communicators may create a tendency of low self-disclosure. McCallister's conceptualisation is based on her long years of experiences. Some differences with McCallister's observation that Reflectives openly engage in personal self-disclosure and Nobles rarely engage in it may be attributed to cultural differences and the methodology used in this study.

Results indicate that college students tend to disclose more about their masculine traits and behaviours to different target groups: male friend, female friend, than about feminine traits and behaviours. It is worthwhile to mention, at this context, that irrespective of biological sex, people prefer to disclose more about their masculine characteristics. These findings are consistent with social expectations where masculine traits are given more importance than feminine traits. Lott (1987) and Miller (1986) argue that in a powerless societal position, women find themselves responsive to the prevailing masculine way of thinking and doing.

In the next hypothesis, it was expected that individuals with high masculine self-disclosure would differ significantly from those with low masculine self-disclosure on their communication styles. Results reveal that high and low groups of masculine self-disclosure differ on noble and socratic communication styles, whereas they do not differ on reflective communication style. Descriptive indices of data indicate that respondents with high masculine self-disclosure prefer noble and those with low self-disclosure prefer reflective communication style. The other hypothesis based on self-disclosure that individuals with high feminine self-disclosure would differ significantly from those with low feminine self-disclosure on communication styles also yields similar findings. Results of this hypothesis have revealed that high and low groups of feminine self-disclosure differ on noble and socratic communication styles, whereas they fail to differ on reflective communication style. Mean scores indicate that respondents with high feminine self-disclosure prefer noble and those with low feminine self-disclosure prefer reflective communication style.

Gudykunst and Ting-Toomey (1988) have observed that self-disclosure is usually associated with direct communication style that is predominant in individualistic cultures, rather than with the indirect communication style that predominates in collectivistic cultures. Observations of Gudykunst and Ting-Toomey (1988) partially support the present findings, as noble communicators are direct and straightforward and have a high level of self-disclosure. Noble communicators possess certain personality characteristics that are expected in individualistic cultures. Thus, it is evident that individuals with high self-disclosure tend to have noble and those with low self-disclosure tend to have reflective communication style.

It was further hypothesized that self-disclosure with friends as compared to parents would predict significantly the communication style. Results reveal that individuals who disclose more about their masculine traits and behaviours with male friends predict noble communication style and individuals who disclose more about their feminine traits and behaviours with male friends predict reflective communication style. Thus, out of four target groups, disclosure with male friends has significant prediction for communication styles. The question that arises is: why does self-disclosure with male friends affect communication style? This may be due to the cultural influence where males are in the dominating position. Pearson, West and Turner (1995) have observed that men and women reinforce traditional sex-role stereotypes where men are in a dominant position as compared to women. Researchers have also observed the influence of self-disclosure on friends. Disclosure with female friends usually focuses on person or family topics, and these topics are more emotional in nature (Haas & Sherman, 1982). Pearson (1993) reports that college students disclose more to their best same-sex friend than to either one of their parents. The present finding gets some support from Pearson's observation. Disclosures between male-male friendships have originally been studied by Tiger (1969) who believe that men form some sort of bond, that is linked to them being male. Males find it difficult to reveal their emotions (Derlega, Metts, Petronio & Margolis, 1993) and are taught to hold back their emotional experiences (Doyle, 1991; Herzberger & Tennen, 1985; Lewis, 1986). Family relationships have also been examined for patterns of self-disclosure. In general, children of either sex tend to self-disclose more to their mothers than to their fathers (Balswick & Balkwell, 1977; Jourard & Lasakow, 1958). However, fathers appear to be the recipients of more accurate disclosures (Woodyard & Hines, 1973). The relationship oriented communication style and high level of self-disclosure is common among women (Aries, 1987; Tannen, 1990). Tannen (1986) states that self-disclosure and shared values are essential to intimacy and are deeply influenced by cultural and ethnic norms. Ethnic groups can be characterized by the way they value and express self-disclosure. Thus, the effect of self-disclosure with male friends on communication styles found in the present study is consistent with other researches. Through survey of literature it becomes obvious that self-disclosure has a great impact on the individual's communication style.

## III

## SELF-ESTEEM AND COMMUNICATION STYLES

It was hypothesized that self-esteem would affect the communication styles. The stepwise regression analysis confirms that individuals with low self-esteem tend to have reflective communication style. Thus, the findings imply that individuals with high level of self-esteem would prefer noble or socratic communication style. Steinem (1992) believes that our culture has an impact on self-esteem. Change in self-esteem may result in changes in our behaviours including our communication style. As suggested by McCallister (1994), Reflectives are passive and non-assertive communicators. They are more often verbally attacked because the other person knows the Reflectives will back down. The ability to be decisive and directive, when necessary, constitutes problem areas that can prevent the Reflectives from achieving personal and professional goals. Reflectives are not viewed as credible communicators because of their soft-spoken, unassertive and non-committal style. In addition, the tendency to say what the other person wants to hear instead of what the Reflectives really feel establishes them as dishonest or devious persons in the eyes of the other. These personality characteristics of Reflectives as proposed by McCallister support the view that Reflectives seem to have low level of self-esteem. On the other hand, individuals with high self-esteem possess certain personality characteristics that are consistent with McCallister's noble or socratic communication style.

The hypothesis based on self-esteem states that high and low groups of individuals on self-esteem would differ significantly on their communication styles. Before testing this hypothesis, it has been examined whether males and females differ on their self-esteem in the present study. Results indicate that males and females do not differ significantly on self-esteem.

Some research findings on self-esteem, however, indicate that males and females differ on their self-esteem. Josephs, Markus and Tafarodi (1992) report that women typically are more likely to have a "collectivist, ensembled, or connected" scheme for their selves, whereas men are more likely to develop an "individualistic, independent or autonomous" scheme for their selves. In her book on self-esteem, Steinem (1992) has noted that in her travels, she encountered so many women who were "smart, courageous and valuable [and yet], who did not think they were smart, courageous or valuable" (p. 3). She claims that women are often the targets of self-help materials, which offer ways to improve self-esteem. DeFrancisco and Allison (1992) have explained this trend by saying, "women's self-esteem is portrayed as women's fault and women's responsibility to correct" (p. 5).

Lott (1987) and Miller (1986) note that low self-esteem in women is a predictable consequence of women's socialization, since girls learn early that they will be less important, less powerful and less effective than men. The self-esteem of men and women may also be affected by others' perceptions of their worth. However, this is not always the case. Although there is a tendency for males to have a stronger sense of self-worth, the difference is slight and the findings are mixed (Pearson, West & Turner, 1995). The present findings go along with the findings of other researchers like Pearson *et al.* (1995) who have reported that although there is a tendency for males to have a stronger sense of self-worth, the difference has been very small.

Although no sex difference is evident on self-esteem in the present study, high and low groups of individuals differ significantly on socratic and reflective communication styles. However, groups do not differ on noble communication style. Descriptive indices of high and low groups of self-esteem on communication styles indicate that individuals high on self-esteem tend to have noble, whereas individuals low on self-esteem tend to have reflective communication style.

Janis and Field (1959) report that individuals with low self-esteem are easier to persuade than those with high self-esteem. Persons with low self-esteem are conformists by nature. They have little confidence in their own opinions and are persuaded easily by someone else's ideas. Individuals with high self-esteem have greater confidence in their own opinions and find it easier to challenge the ideas of others. This makes them less susceptible to persuasion (Burgoon, Hunsaker & Dawson, 1994). The findings of Burgoon, Hunsaker and Dawson go along with the present findings. McCallister's conceptualization of communication styles also corroborates the present findings. According to McCallister, Reflectives can easily be persuaded, whereas Nobles have greater confidence in their opinions and find it easier to challenge the ideas of others. They cannot be easily persuaded. It is to be noted that individuals with high self-esteem may confidently state an opinion even without sufficient evidence, whereas individuals with low self-esteem would hesitate in supporting unproven viewpoints.

Thus, findings on self-esteem of men and women and communication styles are of mixed nature. Some researchers have found no difference in the levels of self-esteem of men and women (e.g., Drummond, McIntire & Ryan, 1977; E.E. Maccoby & Jacklin, 1974) whereas others have noted such differences (e.g., DeFrancisco & Allison, 1992; Gold, Brush & Sprotzer, 1980; Kimball & Gray, 1982; Steinem, 1992). This inconsistency in findings may be due to developmental differences, different standards, gender role, and different types of self-esteem. Setting aside these confounding effects, one may, however, be confirmed that the way people see and communicate with us affects our self-esteem, and self-esteem in turn, affects our communication.

## Limitations of the Present Study and Suggestions for Future Research

While the findings of the present study are informative, some limitations must be acknowledged. This study has been conducted on the self-perception of the respondents. Respondents have reported their self-perceptions about gender role, self-disclosure and self-esteem. There might be some discrepancy, if the respondents report about others. Therefore, it is suggested that future research should focus on this apparent discrepancy in the perceptions of self and others. The multidimensional concept of communication style may also be considered in future studies. Primarily, this study attempts to identify self-perception of a predominant communication style. Context and situation that have not been addressed systematically can provide directions for further research. This study may be just a beginning, as not much attempt has been made to do research in this area in India. The impact of sex differences, gender role differences, self-disclosure and self-esteem on communication styles might be studied in different contexts, for example, informal or formal, familiar or unacquainted, intimate or non-intimate and dyadic or small groups.

Besides gender role self-perception, two other variables have been used in this study, namely, self-disclosure, and self-esteem. Other scales on self-disclosure may be used to measure the self-disclosure of a person, for example, the relational disclosure scale, the emotional self-disclosure scale, etc. Similarly, other types of self-esteem of individuals like specific (academic) self-esteem, social self-esteem, etc. can also be tested. McCallister has proposed six communication styles, out of which the present study deals with only three dominant communication styles. Further researches might be conducted by using all six communication styles on larger samples in a variety of contexts. Context may affect gender related self-evaluation, self-disclosure, self-esteem and communication behaviours.

Age is another factor that might affect the self-perception of a person about gender role and other personality characteristics. Future studies may be carried out with these variables with different age groups like children, adults and older people. It is observed that in many researches, gender role has been used as a predictor variable, paying less attention as to how communication creates gender. So, it is suggested that studies may be carried out to assess the impact of communication on gender. Further, most of the studies on gender and communication have been carried out using between-group designs. Within-group studies like, female-female, male-male communication patterns are other areas of interest in interpersonal communication. Marital communication, social contexts, same sex context, other sex friends, home, workplace, school and situations like social gathering where one does not know many persons are some of the areas of research interest in the field of interpersonal communication for future researches in our country.

The subjects used in this study are college students. They come from different parts of the country, from different types of families, from different home backgrounds and from different income group families. Thus, the findings of the study may be generalized for the student population attending educational institutions in India. Because of regional, economic, language, caste and other socio-cultural differences, these findings cannot be generalized for the total Indian population. Since studies have not been conducted to assess the impact of gender role self-perception, self-disclosure, and self-esteem on communication styles on Indian college students, the present findings cannot be used to compare with similar studies. Conclusions based on this study, therefore, should be considered with caution. Further testing is required using bigger samples of all ages and all social groups from the Indian population.

It is important to note that these findings can be beneficial to training and consulting fields. Students, teachers and other professionals working in the area of interpersonal communication may be greatly benefited. While conducting seminars on communication skills, trainers may emphasize that effective communication is not sex-based. Instead, it is based on gender role, self-disclosure and self-esteem of a person. Our communication pattern with others is deeply rooted with our self-esteem. We can learn more effective techniques when giving presentations, writing memos and conducting meetings by understanding properly the communication behaviours of individuals based on their gender roles. Style is learned and it is not a personality trait that will never change. One style is not better than another. Each style is simply different from the others and has good and bad characteristics. Everyone has the potential to use all three patterns of communication, but people tend to use one pattern predominantly. We can learn and develop these communication styles to make our difficult task easy.

These findings are also useful in interpersonal relations. As observed by Tannen (1990) "the real problem is conversational style. Women and men have different ways of talking" (p. 79). Tannen's reasoning needs to be examined. People having problems in communicating with each other, for example, married couples, students and teachers, father and son, boss and subordinates, etc. may easily get benefited by understanding properly the sex and gender role of individuals.

To sum up, the present findings reveal that gender role self-perceptions affect the self-reported communication styles. Independent of biological sex, these findings indicate that the 'feminine' individuals prefer a sharing, expressive communication style, whereas 'masculine' individuals prefer a dominating, assertive communication style. Further, no interaction is evident between sex and gender role differences. Masculine and feminine self-disclosure has impact on communication styles. Respondents with high masculine and feminine self-disclosure prefer noble communication style, whereas respondents with low masculine and feminine self-disclosure prefer reflective communication style. Individuals with high self-esteem tend to have noble communication style and those with low self-esteem tend to have reflective communication style. Thus, with the present findings, it can be concluded that 'masculine' individuals with high self-disclosure and high self-esteem tend to have noble communication style, whereas 'feminine' individuals with low self-disclosure and low self-esteem tend to have reflective communication style.

# 5

# SUMMARY

The construct of communication style has long been a topic of interest among scholars. The way people perceive themselves interacting and communicating with others is called communication style. Watzlawick, Beavin and Jackson (1967) have defined that communication focuses on the message's interpretation by the receiver and its impact on what is being said and how it is being said. Norton (1978) has identified nine different styles of communication: dominant, dramatic, contentious, animated, impression-leaving, relaxed, attentive, open and friendly. The well developed tool for exploring variations in the way people perceive themselves interacting with others is the Communication Style Profile Test (CSPT) by McCallister (1994). McCallister's conceptualization of communication style, which appears to have evolved from the earlier work of Hart, Carlson and Eadie (1980) and Norton (1978), involves three predominant styles that are labelled: Noble, Socratic and Reflective. The Noble communicator is conceptualized as a direct and straightforward one who feels obligated to state the truth. A Socratic is a verbose, argumentative and analytical communicator who is concerned with details, and a Reflective is a warm, supportive communicator who is concerned with interpersonal relations and the need to avoid conflict. McCallister argues that communication style is acquired through socialization process, and sex differences have nothing at all to do with communication style. Communication Style Profile Test (CSPT) is a unique test and the present study is to assess empirically the impact of gender role self-perception, self-disclosure, and self-esteem on three dominant communication styles as proposed by McCallister.

Researchers in the past three decades tried to examine biological sex differences in communication. During the first wave of research, a number of differences in communication were determined (Bostrom

& Kemp, 1968). This work on sex differences in communication proceeded until 1974, when Bem (1974) introduced the concept of androgyny, the internalization of both masculine and feminine characteristics. Kirtley and Weaver (1999) argue that gender role self-perception is the key factor underlying our attitudes, beliefs and behaviours when interacting and communicating with others. A variety of models have guided the research on gender and communication. Researchers in the area of gender and communication argue that men and women differ greatly in the way they communicate and interact with others (Aries, 1987; Kramarae, 1989; Lakoff, 1975; Tannen, 1990). Researchers in this field often argue that language is not sex-neutral; it seems to divide, separate, and differentiate women from men (Doyle & Paludi, 1991). Individuals learn to be male or female by learning effective means of communications and social behaviours, which are required for their particular gender. Burleson and Samter (1992) have also found sex differences to be significant in social participation and communication skills.

Numerous scholars in the area of gender and communication have observed the stereotypical role of males and females. Females have been characterized as emotional, passive, gentle, highly talkative and having an abundance of facial expressions. Males, on the other hand, have been characterized as task-oriented, blunt, aggressive, ambitious and independent (Canary, Emmers-Sommer & Faulkner, 1997; Deaux & Lewis, 1983; Doyle & Paludi, 1991; Hall, 1984; Kramarae, 1989; Lindzey & Aronson, 1985; Lott, 1987; Tannen, 1990).

Although there are sex differences in communication, considerable research suggests that these differences may play only a small role in the cognitive and behavioural processes that underlie communication (Wood & Lenze, 1989). Heiss (1991), contrary to stereotypic beliefs, observes that males and females display equal power and dominance through their communication styles in intimate relationships. Wheelen and Verdi (1992) find no stereotypic sex differences in the categories of task, maintenance, or verbal participation. Simkins-Bullock and Wildman (1991) are of the opinion that sex differences do not explain substantial differences in the type of language incorporated in the communication styles of males and females. A meta-analysis conducted by Lustig and Andersen (1990) also suggests no sex differences in the communication pattern.

Thus, the review of literature on gender and communication indicates that the findings in this area are full of contradictions. The present study is, therefore, an effort to investigate the different communication behaviours based on sex and gender role in our culture by using an appropriate method.

Self-disclosure involves individuals conveying information about themselves to others that the others do not know. Usually, self-disclosure is associated with direct communication styles that predominate in individualistic cultures, rather than with the indirect communication styles that predominate in collectivistic cultures (Gudykunst & Ting-Toomey, 1988). Self-disclosure lies at the heart of the process of interpersonal communication. It gives an important indication by which others know what is going on inside the communicators. Communication usually qualifies as self-disclosure when one individual reveals information about the self to another during face-to-face interaction (Duck, Rhutt, Hurst & Strejc, 1991). "Self-disclosure is generally regarded as a process in which relationships proceed from non-intimate to intimate areas of exchange with regard to content" (Gilbert & Horenstein, 1975, p. 317). The review of literature shows that the amount of self-disclosure depends on an individual's personality, culture, beliefs, and attitudes. The present study will assess the impact of masculine and feminine self-disclosure on three dominant communication styles as proposed by McCallister (1994). She states that Nobles rarely engage in personal self-disclosure, whereas Reflectives openly engage in it.

Self-esteem concerns the value we place on the images we have of ourselves. If we add to our self-description that we feel pleased about our career and family responsibilities, and are not disappointed in dealing with difficulties, then we are referring to self-esteem. To a significant degree, self-esteem is influenced by evaluative information received from others (Pearson, West & Turner, 1995). Self-esteem is developed in women and men through their experiences and interactions with others and through cultural messages. Self-esteem is a personality variable that will greatly affect the way a person receives and reacts to a message. Individuals with low self-esteem are generally easier to persuade than those with high self-esteem (Janis & Field, 1959). Persons with low self-esteem are conformists by nature. They have little confidence in their own opinions and are persuaded easily by someone else's ideas. Individuals with high self-esteem have greater confidence in their opinions and find it easier to challenge the ideas of others. This makes them less susceptible to persuasion (Burgoon, Hunsaker & Dawson, 1994). Self-esteem of the sender and the receiver affects communication. Change in self-esteem may result in changes in our behaviours including our communication styles. The present study, therefore, would like to examine the impact of self-esteem on communication styles.

Thus, in the light of the above review of literature and discussion, the following hypotheses have been proposed:

1. Gender role would predict significantly the communication styles.
   (a) Masculine gender role would predict significantly the noble communication style.
   (b) Feminine gender role would predict significantly the reflective communication style.
2. Self-disclosure would predict significantly the communication styles.
3. Self-disclosure with friends as compared to parents would predict significantly the communication styles.
4. Self-esteem would predict significantly the communication styles.
5. Males and females would differ significantly on their communication styles.
6. Communication styles of 'masculine' individuals would differ significantly from those of 'feminine' counterparts.
7. Respondent sex and gender role self-perception would interact to influence the communication styles.
8. Individuals with high masculine self-disclosure would differ significantly from those with low masculine self-disclosure on their communication styles.
9. Individuals with high feminine self-disclosure would differ significantly from those with low feminine self-disclosure on their communication styles.
10. High and low groups of individuals on self-esteem would differ significantly on their communication styles.

The regression analysis confirmed ***hypotheses 1, 2, 3, and 4***. It was found that all the independent variables predicted communication styles, as defined by McCallister (1994). In ***hypothesis 5***, it was expected that communication styles reported by males would differ significantly from those of females. The findings based on univariate tests showed that males and females differed significantly on noble and reflective communication styles, but not on socratic communication style. Descriptive indices indicated that males, as compared to females, scored higher on all three communication styles. It was further observed that both sexes scored higher on noble and lower on reflective communication style. Thus, the present findings indicated that both sexes preferred noble to other communication styles. These findings are consistent with the findings of other researchers who have found no clear sex differences in communication styles. McCallister (1994) has observed no sex differences in communication. Heiss (1991) has found that males and females display equal power and dominance through their communication styles in intimate relationships. Wheelen and Verdi (1992) have observed no stereotypic sex differences in the categories of task, maintenance, or verbal participation. Simkins-Bullock and Wildman (1991) have stated that sex differences do not explain substantial differences in the type of language incorporated in the communication styles of males and females. Lustig and Andersen (1990) have not indicated differences in the communication pattern of males and females. Hyde and Linn (1988) in a meta-analysis have found no sex differences in verbal ability. But there are some researchers who have found sex differences in communication, for example, Canary, Emmers-Sommer and Faulkner, 1997; Deaux and Lewis, 1983; Doyle and Paludi, 1991; Fitzpatrick, Mulac and Dindia, 1995; Hall, 1984; Kramarae, 1989; Lindzey and Aronson, 1985; Lott, 1987; Tannen, 1990.

***Hypothesis 6*** stated that 'masculine' individuals would differ significantly from 'feminine' individuals on communication styles. Results obtained by univariate tests confirmed this hypothesis. These findings based on gender role self-perception and communication styles are consistent with earlier research (e.g., Leaper, 1987; Kirtley & Weaver, 1999). The present findings revealed that, independent of biological sex, the 'masculine' individuals reported a preference for a goal-oriented, assertive and dominant communication style (i.e., noble communication style). On the other hand, the 'feminine' individuals reported a preference for a supportive, caring, and expressive communication style (i.e., reflective communication style). Considering the earlier research (e.g., Berryman-Fink, 1983; Lakoff, 1975; Kramer, 1974; Kramarae, 1989; Simkins-Bullock & Wildman, 1991; Tannen, 1990), the present findings suggested that gender role differences would provide a better explanation for variations in communication styles than sex differences. Thus, sex and gender role are to be understood in a proper perspective before coming to any conclusion on communication behaviours of individuals.

Mean scores of masculinity and femininity on Bem Sex Role Inventory used in the present study indicated that individuals scored higher on femininity traits than on masculinity traits. This trend is contradictory to the findings of Kirtley and Weaver (1999), where individuals have scored higher on masculinity than femininity traits. This type of result may be due to the cultural differences of the two countries. In Indian culture, as compared to American culture, individuals in general tend to have more feminine traits than masculine. On the other hand, in American culture people tend to have more masculine traits than feminine.

The results of gender role and communication styles in the present study are based on the individual's self-perceptions rather than the evaluation of others. It is obvious that the criteria we use when forming perceptions of ourselves might be different from how we perceive others. When we evaluate ourselves, biological sex is generally not a question. But when we encounter other people, their physical and sexual attributes are often the first characteristics we would like to scrutinize. Assessing their gender roles may come much later.

***Hypothesis 7*** revealed non-significant interaction effect between sex and gender role variables. The findings of this study suggested that there was no interaction between sex and gender role self-perception that could influence the communication styles of the respondents. This finding is consistent with the observation of Kirtley and Weaver (1999). Thus, it is evident that, independent of biological sex, gender role differences give a better explanation for understanding the communication styles of individuals.

Results of ***hypotheses 8 and 9*** revealed that individuals with high masculine and feminine self-disclosure differed significantly from those with low masculine and feminine self-disclosure on noble and socratic communication styles, but did not differ on reflective communication style. It is worthwhile to mention here that the college students in the present study tended to disclose more about their masculine traits and behaviours to four target groups: male friend, female friend, father and mother than about feminine traits and behaviours. These findings are consistent with social expectations where masculine traits are given more importance than feminine traits. Lott (1987) and Miller (1986) argue that in a powerless societal position, women find themselves responsive to the prevailing masculine way of thinking and doing. Descriptive indices revealed that individuals with high self-disclosure tended to have noble and those with low self-disclosure tended to have reflective communication style. Gudykunst and Ting-Toomey (1988) observed that self-disclosure is usually associated with direct communication style that is predominant in individualistic cultures, rather than with the indirect communication style that predominates in collectivistic cultures. Observations of Gudykunst and Ting-Toomey (1988) partially support the present findings, as noble communicators are direct and straightforward and have high level of self-disclosure. Noble communicators possess certain personality characteristics that are expected in individualistic cultures. The present findings also indicate that the reflective communicators tend to disclose less about their masculine or feminine traits and behaviours. This low level of self-disclosure in Reflectives seems to be consistent with the personality characteristics as proposed by McCallister (1994). She describes that reflective communicators are passive, non-assertive, and keep quiet rather than say something that would hurt the other person's feelings. McCallister's conceptualisation is based on her long years of experience. Some differences with McCallister's observation that Reflectives openly engage in personal self-disclosure and Nobles rarely engage in it may be attributed to cultural differences and the methodology used in this study.

***Hypothesis 10*** was that high and low groups of individuals on self-esteem would differ significantly on their communication styles. Although no sex differences were evident on self-esteem in the present study, high and low groups of individuals differed significantly on socratic and reflective communication styles. However, groups did not differ on noble communication style. Descriptive indices of high and low groups of self-esteem on communication styles indicated that individuals high on self-esteem tended to have noble, whereas individuals low on self-esteem tended to have reflective communication style. Janis and Field (1959) reported that individuals with low self-esteem were easier to persuade than those with high self-esteem. Burgoon, Hunsaker and Dawson (1994) observed that persons with low self-esteem were conformists by nature. They had little confidence in their own opinions and were persuaded easily by someone else's ideas. Individuals with high self-esteem had greater confidence in their opinions and found it easier to challenge the ideas of others. This made them less susceptible to persuasion. The findings of Burgoon *et al.* (1994) go along with the present findings. McCallister's conceptualization of communication styles also supports the present findings.

While the findings of the present study are informative, some limitations must be acknowledged. This study has been conducted on the self-perception of the respondents. Respondents have reported their self-perceptions about gender role, self-disclosure and self-esteem. There might be some discrepancy, if the respondents report about others. Therefore, it is suggested that future research should focus on the discrepancy in the perceptions of self and others in different contexts, for example, informal or formal, familiar or unacquainted, intimate or non-intimate and dyadic or small groups.

The subjects used in this study are college students. They come from different parts of the country, from different types of families, from different home backgrounds and from different income group families. The findings of the present study may be generalized for the student population attending the educational institutions in India. Because of regional, economic, language, caste and other socio-cultural differences, these findings cannot be generalized for the Indian total population. Conclusions based on this study, therefore, should be considered with caution. Further testing is required using bigger samples of all ages and all social groups from the larger Indian population. Finally, with the present findings, it can be concluded that 'masculine' individuals with high self-disclosure and with high self-esteem tend to have noble communication style, whereas 'feminine' individuals with low self-disclosure and with low self-esteem tend to have reflective communication style.

## Abbreviations used in the Appendices

| | |
|---|---|
| **MSR** | Masculine Sex Role |
| **FSR** | Feminine Sex Role |
| **CSN** | Communication Style Noble |
| **CSS** | Communication Style Socratic |
| **CSR** | Communication Style Reflective |
| **MSDMF** | Masculine Self-Disclosure with Male Friend |
| **MSDFF** | Masculine Self-Disclosure with Female Friend |
| **MSDFA** | Masculine Self-Disclosure with Father |
| **MASMO** | Masculine Self-Disclosure with Mother |
| **FSDMF** | Feminine Self-Disclosure with Male Friend |
| **FSDFF** | Feminine Self-Disclosure with Female Friend |
| **FSDFA** | Feminine Self-Disclosure with Father |
| **FSDMO** | Feminine Self-Disclosure with Mother |
| **SE** | Self-Esteem |

*APPENDIX-A*

## BEM SEX ROLE INVENTORY

### Rotated Factor Matrix

| Item No. | Factor 1 | Factor 2 | Factor 3 |
|---|---|---|---|
| MSR1 | .12259 | .27335 | .20281 |
| MSR4 | –.01832 | .10632 | .53719 |
| MSR7 | –.04507 | .41793 | .15878 |
| MSR10 | .18295 | .44335 | .52547 |
| MSR13 | –.27705 | .51079 | .05438 |
| MSR16 | .08529 | .61361 | .44735 |
| MSR19 | .11677 | .39445 | .25984 |
| MSR22 | –.17868 | .57431 | .26307 |
| MSR25 | .24990 | .44246 | .24988 |
| MSR28 | –.29567 | .44792 | .13315 |
| MSR31 | .10452 | .13327 | .40601 |
| MSR34 | .13600 | .44094 | .00468 |
| MSR37 | .14077 | .29316 | .20775 |
| MSR40 | .02685 | .16841 | .42775 |
| MSR43 | .02062 | .07427 | .45932 |
| MSR46 | –.12864 | .12089 | .27661 |
| MSR49 | .06179 | .65862 | –.39297 |
| MSR52 | .05288 | .52919 | –.05052 |
| MSR55 | .03623 | .49380 | .02159 |
| MSR58 | .04781 | .65065 | .35898 |
| FSR2 | .57424 | .08468 | .08004 |
| FSR5 | .64063 | .03413 | .00663 |
| FSR8 | .61665 | –.01564 | .02176 |
| FSR11 | .47566 | –.01034 | .28524 |

(*Contd.*)

| Item No. | Factor 1 | Factor 2 | Factor 3 |
|---|---|---|---|
| FSR14 | .70762 | .03260 | –.04604 |
| FSR17 | .50920 | .07018 | .05455 |
| FSR20 | .49426 | .26107 | .20108 |
| FSR23 | .57821 | .02350 | .00238 |
| FSR26 | .45135 | –.08633 | .26578 |
| FSR29 | .65998 | –.05371 | –.06145 |
| FSR32 | .08531 | –.35987 | –.14160 |
| FSR35 | .29742 | .23699 | .38460 |
| FSR38 | .19448 | –.17979 | –.58096 |
| FSR41 | –.10701 | .11803 | –.35388 |
| FSR44 | .42366 | –.02570 | .26257 |
| FSR47 | .49889 | –.17158 | –.17479 |
| FSR50 | .10041 | –.07715 | –.36464 |
| FSR53 | .23600 | .06734 | –.07003 |
| FSR56 | .35691 | –.02687 | –.10663 |
| FSR59 | .08513 | –.55185 | .47731 |

*APPENDIX-B*

## COMMUNICATION STYLE PROFILE TEST

### Rotated Factor Matrix

| Item No. | Factor 1 | Factor 2 | Factor 3 | Factor 4 |
|---|---|---|---|---|
| CSN1 | –.14757 | .14979 | –.34465 | .32256 |
| CSN4 | –.23819 | .33765 | –.18762 | .36159 |
| CSN10 | –.09040 | .14257 | –.05667 | .40346 |
| CSN13 | –.06834 | .00572 | –.18531 | .43970 |
| CSN22 | –.19996 | .17805 | .46795 | .18204 |
| CSN25 | .09815 | –.12645 | .23137 | .23758 |
| CSN28 | –.41613 | .05545 | .30172 | .10455 |
| CSN31 | .08803 | .00904 | –.25202 | .46707 |
| CSN34 | .15463 | –.15725 | .06445 | .40404 |
| CSN37 | –.10688 | .02404 | .10924 | .39549 |
| CSN43 | .01567 | .06693 | .12844 | .37124 |
| CSN46 | –.15372 | .00380 | .02440 | .55071 |
| CSN49 | .07071 | .07319 | .12194 | .27696 |
| CSN52 | –.12288 | –.12569 | –.01567 | .35328 |
| CSN55 | .03353 | .16624 | –.11698 | .45966 |
| CSN58 | .02899 | –.13277 | .11983 | .29897 |
| CSS2 | .15503 | .40183 | –.09419 | .19825 |
| CSS5 | .11259 | .20545 | –.10760 | .28282 |
| CSS8 | .01734 | .11965 | –.04478 | .40848 |
| CSS11 | .03678 | .43628 | –.25050 | .26649 |
| CSS14 | .25281 | .38034 | .03679 | .12288 |
| CSS17 | .13026 | .15582 | –.20930 | .19240 |
| CSS23 | –.16750 | .31332 | .36521 | .22027 |
| CSS26 | .11577 | .09930 | .02769 | .21127 |
| CSS29 | .04319 | .49502 | –.21064 | .05142 |
| CSS32 | .10895 | .39460 | –.20540 | .39281 |
| CSS35 | –.01767 | .62022 | .06765 | –.00771 |

(*Contd.*)

| Item No. | Factor 1 | Factor 2 | Factor 3 | Factor 4 |
|---|---|---|---|---|
| CSS38 | –.12561 | .59796 | .03595 | –.00124 |
| CSS41 | –.03227 | .51233 | .23046 | –.06215 |
| CSS47 | .09696 | .44708 | –.06945 | .08797 |
| CSS53 | .03266 | .18431 | .15900 | .39069 |
| CSS56 | –.10397 | .53464 | .11850 | .01230 |
| CSR3 | .43208 | –.25015 | .08796 | –.11586 |
| CSR6 | –.06549 | –.08972 | .58561 | –.07955 |
| CSR12 | .22793 | .06329 | –.00179 | .18932 |
| CSR15 | .70846 | .15096 | –.05895 | .05699 |
| CSR18 | .52438 | –.02953 | .13884 | –.11371 |
| CSR24 | –.03356 | –.08650 | .60018 | .09331 |
| CSR27 | .29596 | .26222 | .28948 | –.13029 |
| CSR30 | .64169 | –.02074 | .11118 | .05483 |
| CSR33 | .05497 | –.03349 | .54759 | .09462 |
| CSR36 | .34646 | –.06259 | .18960 | .03629 |
| CSR42 | .06840 | .19140 | .22203 | .02479 |
| CSR45 | .60699 | .17167 | –.14140 | .02351 |
| CSR48 | .19873 | .00669 | .54039 | –.13676 |
| CSR51 | .67385 | .05387 | .05148 | .06758 |
| CSR54 | .27566 | .14169 | .49233 | –.08761 |
| CSR60 | .08100 | –.04700 | .50693 | .00226 |

*APPENDIX-C (I)*

## THE MASCULINE AND FEMININE SELF-DISCLOSURE SCALE

### Rotated Factor Matrix

| Item No. | Factor 1 | Factor 2 | Factor 3 | Factor 4 | Factor 5 |
|---|---|---|---|---|---|
| MSDMF1 | –.12335 | .06807 | .60720 | .09873 | .25681 |
| MSDFF1 | –.07668 | .66498 | –.02382 | .11234 | .31348 |
| MSDFA1 | .03243 | .01119 | .02329 | .71383 | .23499 |
| MSDMO1 | .41247 | .07867 | –.07513 | .36369 | .28604 |
| MSDMF3 | .06342 | .14365 | .61030 | .15242 | .29737 |
| MSDFF3 | .10181 | .65421 | .16561 | .10738 | .33978 |
| MSDFA3 | .19646 | .06845 | .06940 | .70396 | .27940 |
| MSDMO3 | .60007 | .12106 | .04661 | .29656 | .32269 |
| MSDMF5 | .07437 | .20328 | .63744 | .07085 | .37360 |
| MSDFF5 | .08594 | .67691 | .16154 | .05003 | .32427 |
| MSDFA5 | .25286 | .00239 | .10860 | .56639 | .37613 |
| MSDMO5 | .50313 | .06814 | .00603 | .31114 | .42642 |
| MSDMF7 | .10404 | .14330 | .62046 | .13735 | .22186 |
| MSDFF7 | .18197 | .65017 | .14635 | .01429 | .17196 |
| MSDFA7 | .24498 | .04693 | .12722 | .54194 | .23907 |
| MSDMO7 | .59048 | .08844 | .10278 | .18908 | .29558 |
| MSDMF9 | .09710 | .19385 | .61918 | .29789 | –.11754 |
| MSDFF9 | .07988 | .64416 | .24118 | .17858 | –.10892 |
| MSDFA9 | .33514 | .07123 | .22554 | .62267 | –.08358 |
| MSDMO9 | .67984 | .06443 | .18346 | .26947 | –.02825 |
| MSDMF11 | .11708 | .15465 | .67822 | .21881 | –.28101 |
| MSDFF11 | .11403 | .68507 | .25925 | .13532 | –.25646 |
| MSDFA11 | .36591 | .07710 | .25863 | .56125 | –.31149 |
| MSDMO11 | .63899 | .11183 | .22369 | .26913 | –.21779 |
| MSDMF13 | .13732 | .12196 | .70129 | .07037 | –.14712 |
| MSDFF13 | .18346 | .63958 | .20276 | .00712 | –.08910 |
| MSDFA13 | .36664 | –.02033 | .17835 | .42310 | –.15294 |
| MSDMO13 | .63428 | .05497 | .07537 | .11881 | –.05712 |

*(Contd.)*

| Item No. | Factor 1 | Factor 2 | Factor 3 | Factor 4 | Factor 5 |
|---|---|---|---|---|---|
| MSDMF15 | .10429 | .20101 | .66793 | .11407 | .07992 |
| MSDFF15 | .08289 | .74564 | .15701 | .10301 | .08792 |
| MSDFA15 | .29363 | .07505 | .18568 | .61963 | –.01525 |
| MSDMO15 | .59744 | .13161 | .08624 | .23100 | .07200 |
| MSDMF17 | .05303 | .16212 | .68045 | .09223 | –.11433 |
| MSDFF17 | .10225 | .71888 | .19206 | .05418 | –.02128 |
| MSDFA17 | .33344 | .15153 | .21787 | .59226 | –.10193 |
| MSDMO17 | .69125 | .19402 | .16992 | .22444 | –.01466 |
| MSDMF19 | .15942 | .09626 | .67787 | –.06909 | .02444 |
| MSDFF19 | .29917 | .53130 | .13618 | –.14291 | .05630 |
| MSDFA19 | .44824 | .04255 | .15194 | .29093 | –.00587 |
| MSDMO19 | .74704 | .06468 | .09277 | –.00294 | .08092 |
| MSDMF21 | .03854 | .18033 | .57487 | .11213 | .07294 |
| MSDFF21 | .04314 | .73333 | .07883 | .10574 | –.03869 |
| MSDFA21 | .18308 | .13889 | .05035 | .71036 | –.00844 |
| MSDMO21 | .51346 | .17433 | –.02809 | .33309 | .02802 |
| MSDMF23 | .16098 | .15775 | .65559 | .06426 | –.19671 |
| MSDFF23 | .13844 | .70407 | .20442 | .04149 | –.18301 |
| MSDFA23 | .31212 | .17312 | .11132 | .61847 | –.27559 |
| MSDMO23 | .62476 | .18241 | .07709 | .26216 | –.18195 |
| MSDMF25 | .18870 | .20878 | .66485 | .07511 | –.03622 |
| MSDFF25 | .14622 | .71584 | .20203 | .06733 | –.08736 |
| MSDFA25 | .42404 | .12880 | .16805 | .50037 | –.12075 |
| MSDMO25 | .65191 | .13689 | .11270 | .15696 | –.01859 |
| MSDMF27 | .16096 | .16995 | .60807 | .04023 | –.00243 |
| MSDFF27 | .19138 | .60868 | .21561 | .07102 | .06572 |
| MSDFA27 | .41612 | .08834 | .16409 | .44555 | .03607 |
| MSDMO27 | .66667 | .14469 | .07029 | .09167 | .10427 |
| MSDMF29 | .11929 | .19266 | .57908 | .12960 | –.30543 |
| MSDFF29 | .09471 | .72070 | .11433 | .11743 | –.18833 |
| MSDFA29 | .41174 | .13091 | .14400 | .49236 | –.17965 |
| MSDMO29 | .65656 | .19799 | .08020 | .17039 | –.09255 |

*APPENDIX-C (II)*

## THE MASCULINE AND FEMININE SELF-DISCLOSURE SCALE

### Rotated Factor Matrix

| Item No. | Factor 1 | Factor 2 | Factor 3 | Factor 4 | Factor 5 |
|---|---|---|---|---|---|
| FSDMF2 | –.08219 | .53919 | –.01305 | .05756 | .06006 |
| FSDFF2 | .41830 | –.08787 | –.00060 | .06143 | .05831 |
| FSDFA2 | –.09899 | .05083 | .14632 | .51142 | .19253 |
| FSDMO2 | .00089 | –.01645 | .54339 | .12404 | .16252 |
| FSDMF4 | .19702 | .56131 | .07478 | .17285 | .02095 |
| FSDFF4 | .62829 | .14948 | .05470 | .11388 | .03398 |
| FSDFA4 | .17428 | .12609 | .25867 | .58401 | .06403 |
| FSDMO4 | .19067 | .09172 | .56614 | .29919 | .07500 |
| FSDMF6 | .26269 | .69321 | .10291 | .21992 | –.03391 |
| FSDFF6 | .77141 | .18284 | .09101 | .14657 | –.04771 |
| FSDFA6 | .14015 | .28312 | .23774 | .70109 | –.01161 |
| FSDMO6 | .19672 | .18511 | .64861 | .32659 | –.02082 |
| FSDMF8 | .14418 | .68507 | .06944 | .21336 | .00181 |
| FSDFF8 | .74576 | .14205 | .11362 | .15122 | –.07014 |
| FSDFA8 | .14963 | .20898 | .23249 | .71300 | –.02861 |
| FSDMO8 | .17965 | .09615 | .66965 | .31959 | –.03066 |
| FSDMF10 | .20113 | .71414 | .12451 | .28598 | –.10061 |
| FSDFF10 | .73345 | .24224 | .17310 | .16543 | –.08146 |
| FSDFA10 | .13808 | .20731 | .35040 | .72453 | –.04075 |
| FSDMO10 | .16949 | .16789 | .71519 | .36482 | –.00670 |
| FSDMF12 | .16359 | .68705 | .14922 | .19614 | –.10083 |
| FSDFF12 | .64500 | .28668 | .22538 | .16062 | –.07867 |
| FSDFA12 | .17369 | .25183 | .28995 | .68803 | –.03626 |
| FSDMO12 | .19048 | .17343 | .65211 | .35844 | –.02529 |
| FSDMF14 | .16663 | .69855 | .15044 | .10432 | .06572 |
| FSDFF14 | .75345 | .18868 | .15588 | .03695 | .09889 |
| FSDFA14 | .12668 | .21465 | .32549 | .60153 | .10857 |
| FSDMO14 | .16044 | .13678 | .74303 | .15565 | .10351 |

*(Contd.)*

| Item No. | Factor 1 | Factor 2 | Factor 3 | Factor 4 | Factor 5 |
|---|---|---|---|---|---|
| FSDMF16 | .16293 | .70260 | .10267 | .10199 | .11912 |
| FSDFF16 | .73205 | .18597 | .14673 | .04532 | .15823 |
| FSDFA16 | .13888 | .23211 | .28504 | .60335 | .20003 |
| FSDMO16 | .15096 | .11897 | .67545 | .18726 | .19815 |
| FSDMF18 | .17006 | .69105 | .13032 | .05951 | .14864 |
| FSDFF18 | .76147 | .16555 | .16448 | .05722 | .16457 |
| FSDFA18 | .22762 | .18128 | .25227 | .62641 | .27869 |
| FSDMO18 | .16346 | .14971 | .66447 | .21749 | .28453 |
| FSDMF20 | .23199 | .71907 | .16186 | .10769 | .03341 |
| FSDFF20 | .74610 | .19372 | .18274 | .08403 | .06883 |
| FSDFA20 | .13554 | .23746 | .34329 | .59779 | .13443 |
| FSDMO20 | .15303 | .17886 | .70689 | .19529 | .12925 |
| FSDMF22 | .06448 | .55005 | .03399 | .13294 | .34643 |
| FSDFF22 | .62326 | .03790 | .07661 | .09934 | .40351 |
| FSDFA22 | .06419 | .10103 | .16966 | .59281 | .40367 |
| FSDMO22 | .09363 | .03776 | .47781 | .25502 | .42530 |
| FSDMF24 | .17775 | .74132 | .18856 | .14080 | –.02697 |
| FSDFF24 | .73010 | .24292 | .22913 | .14009 | –.00777 |
| FSDFA24 | .18640 | .22564 | .35988 | .66764 | .05825 |
| FSDMO24 | .14026 | .17446 | .73109 | .28919 | .03923 |
| FSDMF26 | –.01053 | .43038 | .09276 | .04027 | .47994 |
| FSDFF26 | .39691 | .06228 | .16536 | .03456 | .52654 |
| FSDFA26 | .03272 | –.01029 | .15200 | .45494 | .54773 |
| FSDMO26 | .06866 | –.04974 | .39909 | .17633 | .55330 |
| FSDMF28 | .08249 | .48826 | .00961 | .07705 | .50643 |
| FSDFF28 | .55472 | .02760 | .03203 | .00638 | .50435 |
| FSDFA28 | .04587 | .12355 | .09581 | .48914 | .56404 |
| FSDMO28 | .04913 | .06903 | .44461 | .10670 | .51991 |
| FSDMF30 | .14839 | .69829 | .13946 | .22488 | .12140 |
| FSDFF30 | .73299 | .19315 | .21844 | .13658 | .06322 |
| FSDFA30 | .17410 | .18885 | .30211 | .67207 | .14337 |
| FSDMO30 | .20984 | .10526 | .60342 | .29116 | .10861 |

*APPENDIX-D*

## ROSENBERG SELF-ESTEEM SCALE

### Rotated Factor Matrix

| Item No. | Factor 1 | Factor 2 |
|---|---|---|
| SE1 | .72603 | .21399 |
| SE2 | .56767 | .22512 |
| SE3 | .73435 | .18640 |
| SE4 | .64108 | –.09010 |
| SE5 | –.08301 | .78995 |
| SE6 | .37091 | .66500 |
| SE7 | .55038 | .32586 |
| SE8 | .67921 | .11237 |
| SE9 | .50345 | .42711 |
| SE10 | .72940 | .10439 |

*APPENDIX-E*

Dear Respondent,

I have been doing research in the area of *Interpersonal Communication*. Presently, I am at the stage of collecting data. For this, I have selected some persons whose views I consider valuable. You are one of those persons and, therefore, I request you to kindly go through the questionnaires attached herewith and give your response as per instructions. Questionnaires consist of *Four Parts* and it will not take more than 50 minutes for you in giving all the responses. Since there is no right or wrong answer for any of the items, you can express your opinion frankly. I assure you that the views expressed by you will be used exclusively for academic purpose.

Thanking you for your kind cooperation,

Yours sincerely,
Vijai N. Giri
Dept. of Humanities & S.S.
IIT, Kharagpur

---

**General Information**

Date:

1. Name of the respondent ______________________ 2. Age ______

3. Roll No. ____________ 4. Dept./Centre ________________

5. Name of the state you come from ____________

Please put a tick mark [✓]

6. Sex [ ] Male 7. Category [ ] Undergraduate

[ ] Female [ ] Postgraduate

8. Type of family you come from [ ] Nuclear

[ ] Joint

9. Your home background [ ] Rural

[ ] Semi-Urban
[ ] Urban

10. Monthly income of your family [ ] Below Rs.10,000

[ ] Between Rs.10,000 and Rs.20,000

[ ] Above Rs.20,000

## Part I

### Instructions

"A number of personality characteristics are given below. Please use these characteristics to describe yourself by writing the appropriate number in the box against each item, on a scale from 5 to 1. We would like to know how true of you each of these characteristics is. Please do not leave any characteristic unmarked".

| Always or almost true | Very often true | Sometimes true | Rarely true | Never or almost never true |
|---|---|---|---|---|
| 5 | 4 | 3 | 2 | 1 |

| Sl. No | Items | Ratings | Sl. No | Items | Ratings |
|---|---|---|---|---|---|
| 1. | Defend my own beliefs ** | | 31. | Self-reliant** | |
| 2. | Affectionate | | 32. | Yielding** | |
| 3. | Conscientious | | 33. | Helpful | |
| 4. | Independent | | 34. | Athletic | |
| 5. | Sympathetic | | 35. | Cheerful | |
| 6. | Moody | | 36. | Unsystematic | |
| 7. | Assertive | | 37. | Analytical** | |
| 8. | Sensitive to needs of others | | 38. | Shy | |
| 9. | Reliable | | 39. | Inefficient | |
| 10. | Strong personality | | 40. | Make decisions easily | |
| 11. | Understanding | | 41. | Flatterable** | |
| 12. | Jealous | | 42. | Theatrical | |
| 13. | Forceful | | 43. | Self-sufficient | |
| 14. | Compassionate | | 44. | Loyal | |
| 15. | Truthful | | 45. | Happy | |
| 16. | Have leadership abilities | | 46. | Individualistic** | |
| 17. | Eager to soothe hurt feelings | | 47. | Soft-spoken | |
| 18. | Secretive | | 48. | Unpredictable | |
| 19. | Willing to take risks** | | 49. | Masculine | |
| 20. | Warm | | 50. | Gullible** | |
| 21. | Adaptable | | 51. | Solemn | |
| 22. | Dominant | | 52. | Competitive | |
| 23. | Tender | | 53. | Childlike** | |
| 24. | Conceited | | 54. | Likeable | |
| 25. | Willing to take a stand | | 55. | Ambitious | |
| 26. | Love children | | 56. | Do not use harsh language** | |
| 27. | Tactful | | 57. | Sincere | |
| 28. | Aggressive | | 58. | Act as a leader | |
| 29. | Gentle | | 59. | Feminine | |
| 30. | Conventional | | 60. | Friendly | |

** Deleted in the process of adaptation

## Part II

### Instructions

"Please read the following statements. Think of the way you *actually* communicate (not the way you should have communicated). Five options are given against each statement ranging from *Almost Always* to *Almost Never*. Put a tick mark (✓) in the appropriate box given against each item. Please do not leave any statement unmarked."

| Sl. No | Statements | Almost Always | Very often | Some-times | Rarely | Almost Never |
|---|---|---|---|---|---|---|
| | | 5 | 4 | 3 | 2 | 1 |
| 1. ** | I am direct, straightforward, frank, and spontaneous when I talk. | | | | | |
| 2. | I think words are very important, and I enjoy using them. | | | | | |
| 3. ** | I am willing to listen to another person, but I really don't like to give advice on what to do. | | | | | |
| 4. | I tend to give my opinions on issues openly. | | | | | |
| 5. ** | I really like to sit and talk with other people. | | | | | |
| 6. | I often feel frustrated because I don't actually say what I really feel. | | | | | |
| 7. ** | I do not tell others about my personal feelings. | | | | | |
| 8. | I view argumentation as a constructive activity. | | | | | |
| 9. ** | Other people tend to tell me their problems. | | | | | |
| 10. | I tend to say what I think, and I expect the other person to do the same. | | | | | |
| 11. | I enjoy debating and discussing different issues. | | | | | |
| 12. ** | I don't feel obligated to state my opinion when I am talking with someone with whom I disagree. | | | | | |
| 13. | I tend to be a "tell it like it is" person. | | | | | |

(*Contd.*)

| | 5 | 4 | 3 | 2 | 1 |
|---|---|---|---|---|---|
| 14. ** Instead of just telling someone my opinion, I tend to lead the person through a series of questions and answers to help him or her reach or understand my conclusion. | | | | | |
| 15. I am polite, supportive, and warm when I talk. | | | | | |
| 16. ** I tend to avoid long discussions that involve a lot of details. | | | | | |
| 17. ** I am very exact and detailed when I tell someone how to go about doing something. | | | | | |
| 18. I will withhold my opinion if I feel expressing it will generate conflict. | | | | | |
| 19. ** I tend to say what I have to say in as few words as possible. | | | | | |
| 20. ** Sometimes it appears that people tune me out when I am talking. | | | | | |
| 21. ** I like to reflect on things for a while before making a final decision. | | | | | |
| 22. I tend to make a lot of "you should" statements. | | | | | |
| 23. ** I tend to give other people advice on what they should do. | | | | | |
| 24. Other people tend to interrupt me when I am speaking. | | | | | |
| 25. ** There is a right and wrong way to do most things. | | | | | |
| 26. ** In any given situation, there are usually many alternatives from which to choose. | | | | | |
| 27. ** I will laugh at unfunny joke to make the joke teller feel better. | | | | | |
| 28. I tend to be impatient when listening to others. | | | | | |
| 29. I have an excellent ability to recall details. | | | | | |
| 30. I will simply keep quiet rather than say something that will hurt the other person's feelings. | | | | | |

(*Contd.*)

| | 5 | 4 | 3 | 2 | 1 |
|---|---|---|---|---|---|
| 31. If I think my friend is making a mistake, I will tell him or her what I think. | | | | | |
| 32. I enjoy analyzing all of the various aspects and details in a given situation. | | | | | |
| 33. I have very good ideas, but my suggestions are often ignored. | | | | | |
| 34. I don't like to argue a position, but if I am sure I'm right, it is important that the other person should know he or she is wrong. | | | | | |
| 35. I tend to explain things by using anecdotal stories and hypothetical examples. | | | | | |
| 36. ** I do not respond to another person who is angry. | | | | | |
| 37. I will interrupt a person who is talking too much. | | | | | |
| 38. I often provide lengthy historical reviews of events and am able to provide names, dates, and the details involved. | | | | | |
| 39. ** I would not tell my friend that he or she has bad breath. | | | | | |
| 40. ** If I receive a lengthy memo, I usually read only the first and last paragraphs and skip over the rest. | | | | | |
| 41. I tend to make if-then-therefore statements (if this happens, then this will happen, therefore, we should...) | | | | | |
| 42. ** I try to show the other person that I am listening by nodding my head and saying, "yes, I see," "uh-huh," and so on. | | | | | |
| 43. ** The first thing I think of is usually what I say. | | | | | |
| 44. ** I seldom make absolute or final statements (e.g. "This will never happen"). | | | | | |

*(Contd.)*

| | | 5 | 4 | 3 | 2 | 1 |
|---|---|---|---|---|---|---|
| 45. | I tend to be a very patient person. | | | | | |
| 46. | If I observe an irritating habit, I tend to tell the other person about it. | | | | | |
| 47. | I enjoy discussing abstract or philosophical concepts. | | | | | |
| 48. | Sometimes I indicate that I agree with the other person even though I really don't. | | | | | |
| 49. ** | I like to deal with the "big picture" and let others deal with the details. | | | | | |
| 50. ** | I get irritated with people who make quick decisions without analyzing all of the details. | | | | | |
| 51. | I am usually soft-spoken. | | | | | |
| 52. ** | I will tell my friend if he or she has bad breath. | | | | | |
| 53. ** | I enjoy trying to persuade another person to accept a position that I support. | | | | | |
| 54. ** | I will tell the other person what he or she wants to hear instead of what I really believe to avoid conflict. | | | | | |
| 55. | I admire people who say exactly what they think. | | | | | |
| 56. | I tend to use a lot of descriptive adjectives and clauses in my written and oral communication. | | | | | |
| 57. ** | I share my personal feelings with others. | | | | | |
| 58. ** | I get irritated with people who are not decisive. | | | | | |
| 59. ** | Sometimes I am accused of being redundant. | | | | | |
| 60. | I tend to "give in" more than other people, and sometimes this bothers me. | | | | | |

** Deleted in the process of adaptation

## Part III

### Instructions

"You have been given a list of 30 items below. The purpose is, to what extent you would like to discuss these items with your *Male Friend, Female Friend, Father* and *Mother*. Four columns are given against each item. You have to write an appropriate number in each column for each item. Please use the following five-point scale ranging from 5 to 1. Do not leave any item unmarked".

| Almost always | Very often | Sometimes | Rarely | Almost never |
|---|---|---|---|---|
| 5 | 4 | 3 | 2 | 1 |

*Example:* Suppose "about your ambition" you would like to discuss only 'Sometimes' with your *Male Friend*, and then write 3 in *Male Friend* column against the item 'about my ambition'.

| Sl. No. | Items | Would like to discuss with: Male friend | Female friend | Father | Mother |
|---|---|---|---|---|---|
| 1. | About my strong beliefs | | | | |
| 2. | About my shyness | | | | |
| 3. | About my self-reliance | | | | |
| 4. | About my loyalty | | | | |
| 5. | About my being independent | | | | |
| 6. | About my sympathetic attitude | | | | |
| 7. | About my assertiveness | | | | |
| 8. | About my tenderness | | | | |
| 9. | About my strong personality | | | | |
| 10. | About my gentleness | | | | |
| 11. | About my leadership abilities | | | | |
| 12. | About my being soft spoken | | | | |
| 13. | About my risk taking behaviour | | | | |
| 14. | About my sensitivity to the needs of others | | | | |

(*Contd.*)

| Sl. No. | Items | Would like to discuss with | | | |
|---|---|---|---|---|---|
| | | Male friend | Female friend | Father | Mother |
| 15. | About my decision making abilities | | | | |
| 16. | About my compassion | | | | |
| 17. | About my efficiency | | | | |
| 18. | About my desire to soothe hurt feelings | | | | |
| 19. | About my aggressiveness | | | | |
| 20. | About my being considerate | | | | |
| 21. | About my ambitions and goals in my work | | | | |
| 22. | About my desire inviting others to talk | | | | |
| 23. | About my competitiveness | | | | |
| 24. | About my kindness | | | | |
| 25. | About my self-sufficiency | | | | |
| 26. | About my desire to visit my relatives | | | | |
| 27. | About my being autonomous | | | | |
| 28. | About my desire to meet old friends | | | | |
| 29. | About my ability to direct a group's activity | | | | |
| 30. | About my being warm | | | | |

## Part IV

### Instructions

"Please read the following statements carefully. Five options ranging from *agree very much* to *disagree very much* are given against each statement. Show your level of agreement by putting a tick mark (✓) in the appropriate box. Please do not leave any item unmarked."

| Sl. No. | Statements | Agree very much | Agree | Neither agree nor disagree | Disagree | Disagree very much |
|---|---|---|---|---|---|---|
| | | 5 | 4 | 3 | 2 | 1 |
| 1. | At times I think I am no good at all. | | | | | |
| 2. | I take a positive attitude towards myself. | | | | | |
| 3. | All in all, I am inclined to feel that I am a failure. | | | | | |
| 4. | I wish I could have more respect for myself. | | | | | |
| 5. | I am able to do things the way most other people can do. | | | | | |
| 6. | I feel that I am a person of worth, at least on an equal plane with others. | | | | | |
| 7. | On the whole, I am satisfied with myself. | | | | | |
| 8. | I feel I do not have much to be proud of. | | | | | |
| 9. | I feel that I have a number of good qualities. | | | | | |
| 10. | I certainly feel useless at times. | | | | | |

## Details of Items on Different Sub-Scales

### Part I. Bem Sex Role Inventory (BSRI)

*(i) Item Nos. on Masculinity Scale:*
1, 4, 7, 10, 13, 16, 19, 22, 25, 28, 31, 34, 37, 40, 43, 46, 49, 52, 55, 58
*(ii) Item Nos. on Femininity Scale:*
2, 5, 8, 11, 14, 17, 20, 23, 26, 29, 32, 35, 38, 41, 44, 47, 50, 53, 56, 59

### Part II. Communication Style Profile Test (CSPT)

*(i) Item Nos. on Noble Communication Style Scale:*
1, 4, 7, 10, 13, 16, 19, 22, 25, 28, 31, 34, 37, 40, 43, 46, 49, 52, 55, 58
*(ii) Item Nos. on Socratic Communication Style Scale:*
2, 5, 8, 11, 14, 17, 20, 23, 26, 29, 32, 35, 38, 41, 44, 47, 50, 53, 56, 59
*(iii) Item Nos. on Reflective Communication Style Scale:*
3, 6, 9, 12, 15, 18, 21, 24, 27, 30, 33, 36, 39, 42, 45, 48, 51, 54, 57, 60

### Part III. The Masculine and Feminine Self-Disclosure Scale (MFSDS)

*(i) Item Nos. on Masculine Self-Disclosure Scale:*
1, 3, 5, 7, 9, 11, 13, 15, 17, 19, 21, 23, 25, 27, 29
*(ii) Item Nos. on Feminine Self-Disclosure Scale:*
2, 4, 6, 8, 10, 12, 14, 16, 18, 20, 22, 24, 26, 28, 30

### Part IV. Rosenberg Self-Esteem Scale (SES)

*Item Nos. on Rosenberg Self-Esteem Scale*
Item Nos. 1 to 10. Scores for item Nos. 1, 3, 4, 8, and 10 were reversed.

# BIBLIOGRAPHY


Altman, I. & Taylor, D. (1973). *Social Penetration. The Development of Interpersonal Relationships*. New York: Holt, Rinehart & Winston.

Aries, E. (1987). "Gender and communication". In P. Shaver & C. Hendrick (Eds.), *Sex and Gender* (pp. 149-176). Newbury Par, CA: Sage.

Ashmore, R.D. & Del Boca, F.K. (1979). "Sex stereotypes and implicit personality theory: Towards a cognitive-social psychological conceptualization". *Sex Roles*, **5**, 219-248.

Baig, T. A. (1976). *India's Women Power*. New Delhi: S. Chand & Co.

Baird, J.E., Jr. (1977). *The Dynamics of Organizational Communication*. New York: Harper and Row.

Bakan, D. (1966). *The Duality of Human Existence*. Chicago: Rand McNally.

Ball, J. M. (1958). "The relationship between the ability to speak effectively and the primary mental abilities, verbal comprehension and general reasoning". *Speech Monographs*, **25**, 285-290.

Balswick, J.O. & Balkwell, J.W. (1977). "Self-disclosure to same- and opposite-sex parents: An empirical test of insights from role theory". *Social Psychology Quarterly*, **40**, 282-286.

Bandura, A. (1986). *Social Foundations of Thought and Action: A Social Cognitive Theory*. Englewood Cliffs, NJ: Prentice-Hall.

Barkar, L. L. (1978). *Communication*. Englewood Cliffs, NJ: Prentice-Hall.

Barnlund, D. (1975). *Public and Private Self in Japan and the United States*. Tokyo: Simul.

Bednar, R.L. Wells, M.G. & Peterson, S.R. (1989). *Self-esteem: Paradoxes and Innovations in Clinical Theory and Practice*. Washington, DC: American Psychological Association.

Bem, S. (1974). "The measurement of psychological androgyny." *Journal of Consulting and Clinical Psychology*, **42**, 155-162.

Bem, S. (1975). "Sex role adaptability: One consequence of psychological androgyny". *Journal of Personality and Social Psychology*, **31**, 634-643.

Bem, S. (1976). "Probing the promise of androgyny". In A.G. Kaplan &

J. P. Bean (Eds.), *Beyond Sex-role Stereotypes: Readings Toward a Psychology of Androgyny* (pp. 48-62). Boston: Brown, Little, and Company.

Bem, S., Martyna, W., & Watson, C. (1976). "Sex typing and androgyny: Further exploration of the expressive domain". *Journal of Personality and Social Psychology,* **34**, 1016-1023.

Bem, S. (1977). "On the utility and alternative procedures for assessing psychological androgyny". *Journal of Consulting and Clinical Psychology*, **45**, 196-205.

Bem, S. (1981). *Bem Sex Role Inventory: Professional Manual*. Palo Alto, CA: Consulting Psychologists Press.

Bem, S. (1985). "Androgyny and gender schema theory: A conceptual and empirical integration". In T.B. Sonderegger (Ed.), *Nebraska Symposium on Motivation: Psychology and Gender* (pp. 179-226). Lincoln: University of Nebraska Press.

Bem, S. (1993). *The Lenses of Gender*. New Haven, CT: Yale University Press.

Berryman-Fink, C. & Wilcox, J. (1983). "A multivariate investigation of perceptual attributions concerning gender appropriateness in language". *Sex Roles*, **9**, 663-681.

Birdwhistell, R.L. (1952). *Introduction to kinesics: An annotation system for analysis of body motion and gesture.* Washington, DC: Foreign Service Institute, U.S. Department of State/Ann Arbor, MI: University Microfilms.

Block, J.H. (1973). "Conceptions of sex role: Some cross-cultural and longitudinal perspectives". *American Psychologist*, **28**, 512-526.

Block, J.H. (1976). "Issues, problems, and pitfalls in assessing sex differences: A critical review of the psychology of sex differences." *Merrill-Palmer Quarterly*, **22**, 283-308.

Bochner, A.P. & Kelly, C.W. (1974). "Interpersonal competence: Rationale, philosophy, and implementation of a conceptual framework." *Speech Teacher*, **23**, 279-301.

Bostrom, R N. & Kemp, A.P. (1968). "Type of speech, sex of speaker, and sex of subject as factors influencing persuasion". *Central States Speech Journal*, **20**, 245-252.

Bradac, J.J., Hosman, L.A., & Tardy, C.H. (1978). "Reciprocal disclosures and language intensity: Attributional consequences". *Communication Monographs*, **45**, 1-17.

Brage, D. & Meredith, W. (1994). "A causal model of adolescent depression". *Journal of Psychology*, **128**, 455-468.

Briton, N.J. & Hall, J.A. (1995). "Beliefs about female and male non-verbal communication." *Sex Roles*, **32**, 79-91.

Bryan, A.I., & Wilke, W. H. (1942). "Audience tendencies in rating public speakers". *Journal of Applied Psychology*, **26**, 371-381.

Burgoon, M., Hunsaker, F.G., & Dawson, E.J. (1994). *Human Communication*. Thousand Oaks, CA: Sage.

Burleson, B., & Samter, W. (1992). "Are there gender differences in the relationship between academic performance and social behaviour?" *Human Communication Research*, **19**,155-175.

Canary, D. J., & Hause, K. S. (1993). "Is there any reason to research sex differences in communication?" *Communication Quarterly*, **41**, 129-144.

Canary, D.J., Emmers-Sommer, T.M., & Faulkner, S. (1997). *Sex and Gender Differences in Personal Relationships*. New York: Guilford Press.

Cegala, D.J. (1981). "Interaction involvement: A Cognitive dimension of communicative competence". *Communication Education*, **30**, 109-121.

Chelune, G.J. (1979). *Self-disclosure: Origins, Pattern, and Implications of Openness in Interpersonal Relationships*. San Francisco: Jossey-Bass.

Coates, J. (1986). *Women, Men, and Language: A Sociolinguistic Account of Sex Differences in Language*. London: Longman.

Coopersmith, S. (1967). *The Antecedents of Self-esteem.* San Francisco: W.H. Freeman and Company.

Das, S. & Ghadially, R. (1996). "Parental sex role orientation and sex stereotypes of children". In R. Ghadially (Ed.), *Women in Indian Society* (pp.124-135). New Delhi: Sage.

De Souza, A. (1975). *Women in Contemporary India*. New Delhi: Manohar Publications.

Deaux, L. & Lewis, D. (1983). "Components of gender stereotypes". *Psychological Documents*, **13**, 2583.

DeFrancisco, V. & Allison, A. (1992). "A feminist Guide to Studying Self-esteem in Communication". Paper presented at the annual conference of the Organization for the Study of Communication, Language, and Gender. Hemstead, NY.

Demo, D.H., Small, S. A., & Savin-Williams, R.C. (1987). "Family relations and the self-esteem of adolescents and their parents." *Journal of Marriage and Family*, **49**, 705-715.

Derlega, V. J., Metts, S., Petronio, S., & Margolis, S.T. (1993). *Self-disclosure.* New Bury Park, CA: Sage.

Dimond, R.E. & Hellkamp, D.T. (1969). "Race, sex, ordinal position of birth, and self-disclosure of high school students." *Psychological Reports,* **25**, 235-238.

Dimond, R.E. & Munz, D.C. (1967). "Ordinal position of birth and self-disclosure of high school students". *Psychological Reports*, **21**, 829-833.

Doyle, J. (1991). *The Male Experience*. Dubuque, IA: William C. Brown.

Doyle, J., & Paludi, M. (1991). *Sex and Gender: The Human Experience*. Dubuque, IA: William C. Brown.

Drummond, R.J., McIntire, W. G., &. Ryan, C.W. (1977). "Stability and sex differences on the Coppersmith self-esteem inventory for students in grades two to twelve". *Psychological Reports*, **40**, 943-946.

Duck, S. & Pittman, G. (1994). "Social and personal relationships". In M.L. Knapp & G.R. Miller (Eds.), *Handbook of Interpersonal Communication* (pp. 676-695). Thousand Oaks: Sage.

Duck, S., Rhutt, D.J., Hurst, M. H. & Strejc. H. (1991). "Some evident truths about conversations in everyday relationships: All communications are not created equal". *Human Communication Research*, **18**, 228-267.

Dukes, R. & Lorch, B. (1989). "Concept of self, mediating factors, and adolescent deviance". *Sociological Spectrum*, **9**, 301-319.

Duran, R.L. (1992). "Communicative adaptability: A review of conceptualization and measurement", *Communication Quarterly*, **40**, 253-268.

Eagly, A.H. (1987). *Sex Differences in Social Behaviour: A Social-role Interpretation*. Hillsdale, NJ: Erlbaum.

Enger, J.M., Howerton, D.L. & Cobbs, C.R. (1993). "Internal/external locus of control, self-esteem, and parental verbal interaction of at-risk black male adolescents". *Journal of Social Psychology*, **134**, 269-274.

Erikson, E. (1964). "Inner and outer space: Reflections on womenhood". In R.J. Lifton (Ed.), *The Women in America*. New York: Houghton Mifflin.

Feeney, J.A., Noller, P., & Callan, V.J. (1994). "Attachment style, communication and satisfaction in the early years of marriage." *Advances in Personal Relationships*, **5**, 269-308.

Feigenbaum, W.M. (1977). "Reciprocity in self-disclosure within the psychological interview". *Psychological Reports*, **40**, 15-26.

Fitzpatrick, M.A., Mulac, A., & Dindia, K. (1995). "Gender-preferential language use in spouse and stranger interaction". *Journal of Language and Social Psychology*, **14**, 18-39.

Franklin, C. M., II. (1984). *The Changing Definition of Masculinity*. New York: Plenum.

Ghadially, R. & Kazi, K.A. (1980). "Sex-role attitudes, marriage and career among college men and women". *Indian Journal of Social Work*, **40**, 441- 447.

Ghanekar, A. (1998). *Communication Skill for Effective Management*. Pune: Everest Publishing House.

Gilbert, S.J. (1976). "Empirical and theoretical extensions of self-disclosure". In G.R. Miller (Ed.), *Explorations in Interpersonal Communication* (pp.197-216). Beverley Hills, CA: Sage.

Gilbert, S.J. & Horenstein, D. (1975). "The communication of self-disclosure: Level versus valence". *Human Communication Research*, **1**, 316-322.

Gilligan, C. (1982). *In a Different Voice: Psychological Theory and Women's Development*. Cambridge, MA: Harvard University Press.

Gold, A.R., Brush, L.R., & Sprotzer, E.R. (1980). "Developmental changes in self-perceptions of intelligence and self-confidence". *Psychology of Women Quarterly*, **5**, 231-239.

Gorsuch, R.L. (1983). *Factor Analysis*. Hillsdale, NJ: Lawrence Erlbaum.

Gray, J. (1992). *Men are from Mars, women are from Venus: A Practical Guide for Improving Communication and Getting what you want in Your Relationships*. New York: Harper Collins.

Greenblatt, L., Hasenauer, J. E., &. Freimuth, V. S. (1980). "Psychological sex type and androgyny in the study of communication variables: Self-disclosure and communication apprehension". *Human Communication Research*, **6**, 117-129.

Gudykunst, W.B. & Lim, T. (1985). "Ethnicity, sex and self-perception of communicator style". *Communication Research Report*, **2**, 68-75.

Gudykunst, W.B., Yoon, Y., & Nishida, T. (1987). "The influence of individualism-collectivism on perceptions of communication in ingroup and outgroup relationships". *Communication Monographs*, **54**, 295-306.

Gudykunst, W.B. & Ting-Toomey, S. (1988). *Culture and Interpersonal Communication*. Newbury Park, CA: Sage.

Haas, A. & Sherman, M. (1982). "Reported topics of conversation among same-sex adults". *Communication Quarterly*, **30**, 332-342.

Hacker, M. (1981). "Blabbermouths and calms: Sex differences in self-disclosure in same-sex and cross-sex friendship dyads." *Psychology of Women Quarterly*, **5**, 385-401.

Hall, E. T. (1959). *The Silent Language*. Garden City, NY: Doubleday.

Hall, J. (1984). *Nonverbal Sex Differences*. Baltimore: John Hopkins Press.

Hally, C. & Pollack, R. (1993). "The effects of self-esteem, variety of sexual experience, and erotophilia on sexual satisfaction in sexually active heterosexuals". *Journal of Sex Education and Therapy*, **19**,183-192.

Hansford, B. & Hattie, J. (1987). "Perceptions of communication style and self-concept". *Communication Research*, **14**, 189-203.

Harris, A.C. (1994). "Ethnicity as a determinant of sex role identity: A replication study of item selection for the Bem Sex Role Inventory". *Sex Roles*, **31**, 241-273.

Hart, R.P. & Burks, D.M. (1972). "Rhetorical sensitivity and social interaction". *Speech Monographs*, **39**, 75-91.

Hart, R.P., Carlson, R.E., & Eadie, W.F. (1980). "Attitudes toward communication and the assessment of rhetorical sensitivity". *Communication Monographs*, **47**, 1-22.

Harter, S. (1993). "Causes and consequences of low self-esteem in children and adolescents". In R.F. Baumeister (Ed.), *Self-esteem: The Puzzle of Low Self-Regard* (pp. 87-116). New York: Plenum Press.

Heider, F. (1958). *The Psychology of Interpersonal Relations*. New York: Wiley.

Heiss, F. (1991). "Gender and romantic-love roles". *Sociological Quarterly*, **32**, 575-591.

Herzberger, S. & Tennen, H. (1985). "Snips and snails and puppy dog tails: Gender of agent, recipient, and observer as determinants of perceptions of discipline." *Sex Roles*, **12**, 853-865.

Holt, C.L. & Ellis, J.B. (1998). "Assessing the current validity of the Bem Sex Role Inventory". *Sex Roles*, **39**, 929-941.

Hoyenga, K.B. & Hoyenga, K.T. (1979). *The Question of Sex Differences: Psychological Cultural and Biological Issues*. Boston: Little Brown.

Huang, L.N. (1999). "Family communication patterns and personality characteristics". *Communication Quarterly*, **47**, 230-243.

Hunt, G.T. (1985). *Effective Communication*. New Jersey: Prentice-Hall, Inc.

Hyde, J.S. & Rosenberg, B.G. (1980). *Half the Human Experience: The Psychology of Women*. Lexington, Mas: D.C. Heath.

Hyde, J.S. & Linn, M.C. (1988). "Gender differences in verbal ability: A meta-analysis". *Psychological Bulletin*, **104**, 53-69.

Jain, D. (1975). *Indian Women*. New Delhi: Government of India.

James, W. (1950). *The Principles of Psychology*. New York: Dover

Publications.

Janis, I.L. & Field, P.B. (1959). "A behavioural assessment of persuasibility". In C.I. Hovland & I.L. Janis (Eds.), *Personality and persuasibility* (pp. 29-54). New Haven, CT: Yale University Press.

Johannesen, R.L. (1971). "The emerging concept of communication as dialogue". *Quarterly Journal of Speech*, **57**, 373-382.

Josephs, R.A., Markus, H.R., & Tafarodi, R.W. (1992). "Gender and self-esteem". *Journal of Personality and Social Psychology*, **63**, 391-402.

Jourard, S.M. & Lasakow, P. (1958). "Some factors in self-disclosure". *Journal of Abnormal and Social Psychology*, **56**, 91-98.

Jourard, S.M. (1959). "Healthy personality and self-disclosure". *Mental Hygiene*, **43**, 499-507.

Jourard, S.M. & Friedman, R. (1970). "Experimenter-subject "distance" and self-disclosure". *Journal of Personality and Social Psychology*, **15**, 278-282.

Jourard, S.M. (1971). *The Transparent Self.* New York: Van Nostrand Reinhold.

Katsurada, E. & Sugihara, Y. (1999). "A preliminary validation of the Bem Sex Role Inventory in Japanese culture". *Journal of Cross-cultural Psychology,* **30**, 641-645.

Keith, D. (1993). *Human Communication at Work*. New Delhi: Tata McGraw-Hill.

Keyton, III. (1999). "Relational communication in groups". In L.R. Frey, D.S. Gouran, & M.S. Poole (Eds.), *The Handbook of Group Communication Theory and Research* (pp. 192-222). Thousand Oaks, CA: Sage.

Kimball, M. & Gray, V.A. (1982). "Feedback and performance expectancies in an academic setting". *Sex Roles*, **8**, 999-1007.

Kirtley, M.D. & Weaver III, J. B. (1999). "Exploring the impact of gender role self-perception on communication style". *Women's Studies in Communication*, **22**, 190-209.

Kitano, H.H. (1989). "Alcohol and drug use and self-esteem: A sociocultural perspective." In A. Mecca, N. Smelser, & J. Vasconcellos (Eds.), *The Social Importance of Self-esteem* (pp. 294-326). Berkeley, CA: University of California Press.

Knapp, M.L., Miller, R.G., & Fudge, K. (1994). "Background and current trends in the study of interpersonal communication". In M.L. Knapp & G.R. Miller (Eds.), *Handbook of Interpersonal Communication* (pp. 3-20). Thousand Oaks: Sage Publications.

Kramarae, C. (1989). "Redefining gender, race, and class". In C. Lont & S. Friedley (Eds.), *Beyond Boundaries: Sex and Gender Diversity in Communication* (pp. 317-330). Fairfax, VA: George Mason University Press.

Kramer, C. (1974). "Women's speech: Separate but unequal?" *Quarterly Journal of Speech*, **60**, 14-24.

Krone, K., Garrett, M., & Chen, L. (1992). "Managerial communication practices in Chinese factories: A preliminary investigation". *Journal of Business Communication*, **29**, 229.

Lakoff, R. (1975). *Language and Woman's Place*. New York: Harper & Row.

Landrine, H. (1985). "Race × class stereotypes of women". *Sex Roles*, **13**, 65-75.

Leaper, C. (1987). "Agency, communion, and gender as predictors of communication style and being liked in adult male-female dyads". *Sex Roles*, **16**, 137-149.

Lewis, C. (1986). *Becoming a Father*. Philadelphia, PA: Open University Press.

Lindsey, A.E. & Zakahi, W.R. (1998). "Perceptions of men and women departing from conversational sex role stereotypes during initial interaction," In D.J. Canary, & K. Dindia (Eds.), *Sex Differences and Similarities in Communication* (pp. 393-412). Mahwah, NJ: Erlbaum.

Lindzey, G. & Aronson, E. (1985). *The Handbook of Social Psychology*. New York: Random House.

Lott, B. (1987). *Women's Lives: Themes and Variations in Gender Learning*. Monterey, CA: Brooks/Cole.

Lustig, M.W. & Andersen, P.A. (1990). "Generalizing about communication apprehension and avoidance: Multiple replications and meta-analysis". *Journal of Social Behaviour and Personality*, **5** (Spec. Issue), 309-340.

Maccoby, D. & Jacklin, C. (1974). *The Psychology of Sex Differences*. Stanford, CA: Stanford University Press.

Maccoby, E.E. & Jacklin, C.N. (1974). "Myth, reality, and shades of gray: What we know and don't know about sex differences". *Psychology Today*, **8** (December), 109-112.

Maccoby, E.E. (1990). "Gender and relationships: A developmental account". *American Psychologist*, **45**, 513-520.

Marche, T.A. & Peterson, C. (1993). "On the gender differential use of listener responsiveness". *Sex Roles*, **29**, 795-817.

McAllister, H.A. (1980). "Self-disclosure and liking: Effects for senders and receivers". *Journal of Personality*, **48**, 409-418.

McCallister, L. (1994). "*I wish I'd said that*!" New York: John Wiley & Sons.

Miller, G. (1951). *Language and Communication*. New York: McGraw-Hill.

Miller, J.B. (1986). *Toward a New Psychology of Women*. Boston, MA: Beacon Press.

Montgomery, B. & Norton, R. (1981). "Sex differences and similarities in communicator style". *Communication Monographs*, **48**, 121-132.

Nanda, B.R. (1976). *Indian Women*. New Delhi: Vikas.

Norton, R. (1977). "Teacher effectiveness as a function of communicator style". In B. Ruben (Ed.), *Communication Yearbook* 1 (pp. 525-542). New Brunswick, NJ: Transaction.

Norton, R. (1978). "Foundation of a communicator style construct". *Human Communication Research*, **4**, 99-112.

Norton, R. (1983). *Communicator Style: Theory, Applications, and Measures*. Beverly Hills, CA: Sage.

Norton, R. (1986). "Communicator style in teaching: Giving form to content". In J. Civikly (Ed.), *Communicating in College Classrooms* (pp. 33-40). San Francisco: Jossey-Bass.

Nunnally, J.C. (1978). *Psychometric Theory*. New York: McGraw-Hill.

Nussbaum, J. & Scott, M. (1979). "The relationship between communicator style, perceived self-disclosure, and classroom learning." In D. Nimmo (Ed.), *Communication Yearbook* 3 (pp. 561-584). New Brunswick, NJ: Transaction.

Nyrop, R.F., Benderly, B.L., Cover, W.W., Cutter, M.J., & Parker, N.B. (1975). *Area Handbook of India*. Washington, D.C.: American University.

O'Keefe, B. (1988). "Three logics of message design: Individual differences in reasoning about communication". *Communication Monographs*, **55**, 80-103.

Parker, R.G. & Parrott, R. (1995). "Patterns of self-disclosure across social support networks: Elderly, middle ages, and young adults". *International Journal of Aging and Human Development*, **41**, 281-297.

Parsons, R., & Bales, R. F. (1955) *Family, Socialization and Interaction Process*. New York: Free Press.

Pearce, W.B. & Sharp, S. M. (1973). "Self-disclosing communication". *Journal of Communication*, **23**, 409-425.

Pearson, J.C. (1980). "Sex roles and self-disclosure". *Psychological*

*Reports*, **47**, 640.

Pearson, J.C. (1993). *Communication in the Family*. New York: Harper Collins.

Pearson, J.C., West, R.L., & Turner, L.H. (1995). *Gender and Communication*. Boston: McGraw Hill.

Pedersen, D.M. & Higbee, K.L. (1969). "Personality correlates of self-disclosure". *Journal of Social Psychology*, **78**, 81-89.

Petronio, S. (1991). "Communication boundary management: A theoretical model of managing disclosure of private information between marital couples". *Communication Theory*, **1**, 311-335.

Philips, S.U., Steele, S., & Tanz, C. (Eds.) (1987). *Language, Gender, and Sex in Comparative Perspective*. New York: Cambridge University Press.

Pruett, B.M. (1989). "Male and female communicator style differences: A meta analysis". In C.M. Lont & S.A. Friedley (Eds.), *Beyond Boundaries: Sex and Gender Diversity in Communication* (pp. 107-120). Fairfax, VA: George Mason University Press.

Rao, V. V. P. & Rao, N.V. (1996). "Sex role attitudes of college students in India". In R. Ghadially (Ed.), *Women in Indian Society* (pp. 109-123). New Delhi: Sage.

Rogers, C.R. (1951). *Client-centered Therapy*. Boston: Houghton Mifflin.

Rosenberg, M. (1989). *Society and the Adolescent Self-image*. Middletown, CT: Wesleyan University Press.

Rosenberg, M., Schooler, C. (1989). "Self-esteem and adolescent problems: Modelling reciprocal effects". *American Sociological Review*, **54**, 1004-1018.

Rosenberg, M., Schooler, C., Schoenbach, C., & Rosenberg, F. (1995). "Global self-esteem and specific, self-esteem: Different concepts, different outcomes". *American Psychological Review*, **60**, 141-159.

Ruesch, J. & Bateson, G. (1951). *Communication: The Social Matrix of Psychiatry*. New York: W. W. Norton.

Sethi, R.R. & Allen, M.J. (1996). "Sex role stereotypes in Northern India and the United States". In R. Ghadially (Ed.), *Women in Indian Society* (pp. 99-108). New Delhi: Sage.

Sheldon, A. (1993). "Pickle fights: Gendered talk in preschool disputes". In D. Tannen (Ed.), *Gender and Conversational Interaction* (pp. 83-109). New York: Oxford University Press.

Simkins-Bullock, F. & Wildman, B. (1991). "An investigation into the relationships between gender and language". *Sex Roles*, **24**, 149-160.

Simmel, G. (1950). *The Sociology of George Simmel*. New York: Free Press

Singh, R. & Lele, J.K. (1990). "Language, power, and cross-sex communication strategies in Hindi and Indian English revisited." *Language and Society*, **19**, 541-546.

Snell, W.E., Jr., Belk, S.S., & Hawkins, R.C. II. (1986). "The Masculine and Feminine Self-Disclosure Scale: The politics of masculine and feminine self-presentation". *Sex Roles*, **15**, 249-267.

Snell, W.E., Jr., Belk, S.S., Flowers, A. & Warren, J. (1988). "Women and men's willingness to self-disclose to therapists and friends: The moderating influence of instrumental, expressive, masculine, and feminine topics". *Sex Roles*, **18**, 769-776.

Snell, W.E., Jr., Miller, R.S. & Belk, S.S. (1988). "Development of the Emotional Self-Disclosure Scale". *Sex Roles*, **18**, 59-73.

Snell, W.E., Jr., Miller, R.S., Belk, S.S., Garcia-Falconi, R., & Hernandez-Sanchez, J.E. (1989). "Men's and women's emotional disclosures: The impact of disclosure recipient, culture, and the masculine role". *Sex Roles*, **21**, 467-486.

Snell, W.E., Jr. (1989). "Willingness to self-disclose to female and male friends as a function of social anxiety and gender". *Personality and Social Psychology Bulletin*, **15**, 113-125.

Snoek, D. & Rothblum, E. (1979). "Self-disclosure among adolescents in relation to parental affection and control patterns." *Adolescence*, **14**, 333-340.

Stamp, G.H.C. (1999). "A qualitatively constructed interpersonal communication model: A grounded theory analysis". *Human Communication Research*, **25**, 531-547.

Steinem, G. (1992). *Revolution from Within: A Book of Self-esteem*. Boston: Little, Brown & Co.

Sugihara, Y. & Katsurada, E. (1999). "Masculinity and femininity in Japanese culture: A pilot study". *Sex Roles*, **40**, 635-646.

Talley, M.A. & Richmond, V.P. (1980). "The Relationship between psychological gender orientation and communicative style". *Human Communication Research*, **6**, 326-339.

Tannen, D. (1986). *That's not what I meant! How Conversational Style Makes or Breaks Your Relations with Others*. New York: William Morrow & Company.

Tannen, D. (1990). *You Just Don't Understand: Women and Men in Conversation*. New York: William Morrow & Company.

Tardy, C.H., Hosman, L.A., & Bradac, J.J. (1981). "Disclosing self to friends and family: A re-examination of initial questions". *Communication Quarterly*, **29**, 263-268.

Taylor, D. A. (1965). "Some aspects of the development of interpersonal relationships: Social penetration process". *Technical Report No. I*. Center for Research on Social Behaviour: University of Delaware.

Thayer, L. (1963). "On theory building in communication I. Some conceptual problems". *Journal of Communication*, **13**, 43.

Thompson, B. & Daniel, L.G. (1996). "Factor analytic evidence for the construct validity of scores: A historical overview and some guidelines". *Educational and Psychological Measurement*, **56**, 197-208.

Thorne, B., Kramarae, C., & Henley, N. (Eds.) (1983). *Language, Gender and Society*. Rowley, M.A.: Newbury House.

Thornstam, L. (1992). Loneliness in marriage. *Journal of Social and Personal Relationships*, **9**, 197-217.

Tiger, L. (1969). *Men in Groups*. New York: Random House.

Vangelisti, A.L. (1998). "Miscommunication". *The Quarterly Journal of Speech*, **84**, 255-256.

Verdman, G.T. (1970). *Effective Communication of Ideas*. New York: Van Nostrand Reinhold Company.

Ward, C. & Sethi R.R. (1986). "Cross-cultural validation of the Bem Sex Role Inventory: Malaysia and South Indian research". *Journal of Cross-cultural Psychology*, **17**, 300-314.

Watzlawick, P., Beavin, J., & Jackson, D. (1967). *Pragmatics of Human Communication: A Study of Interpersonal Patterns, Pathologies and Paradoxes*. New York: Norton Company.

Weaver, J.B. III., Fitch-Hauser, M., Villaume, W., & Thomas, T. (1993). "Exploring the impact of gender-role schematicity on communication anxiety". Presented before the Speech Communication Association, Miami, FL.

Wheelen, S. & Verdi, A. (1992). "Differences in male and female patterns of communication in groups: A methodological artifact?" *Sex Roles*, **27**, 1-15.

Whiting, B. & Edwards, C.P. (1973). "A cross-cultural analysis of sex differences in the behaviour of children aged three through eleven". *Journal of Social Psychology*, **91**,171-188.

Winstead, B.A. (1986). "Sex differences in same-sex friendships". In V. Derlega & B.A. Winstead (Eds.), *Friendship and Social Interaction*. New York: Springer-Verlag.

Wood, J. (1994). *Who Cares? Women, Care and Culture*. Edwardsville, IL: South Illinois University.

Wood, J. & Lenze, L. (1989). "Gender and the development of self:

Inclusive pedagogy in interpersonal communication". *Women's Studies in Communication*, **14**, 1-23.

Woodyard, H.P. & Hines, D.A. (1973). "Accurate compared to inaccurate self-disclosure". *Journal of Humanistic Psychology*, **13**, 61-67.

Worthy, M.A., Gary, I., & Kahn, G.M. (1969). "Self-disclosure as an exchange process". *Journal of Personality and Social Psychology*, **13**, 59-63.

Wylie, R.C. (1961). *The Self-concept: A Critical Survey of Pertinent Research Literature.* Lincoln, NE: University of Nebraska Press.

Zillman, D., Weaver, J.B., Mundorf, N., & Aust, C.F. (1986). "Effects of opposite-gender companion's affect to horror on distress, delight, and attraction". *Journal of Personality and Social Psychology*, **51**, 586-594.

Zimbardo, R. (1977). *Shyness: What it is; What to do About it.* New York: Ballentine.

# Index